Kashmir Conflict Detail

Law and Abuse.

Author
Melbourne Marsh

Copyright Notice

Copyright © 2017 Global Print Digital
All Rights Reserved

Digital Management Copyright Notice. This Title is not in public domain, it is copyrighted to the original author, and being published by **Global Print Digital**. No other means of reproducing this title is accepted, and none of its content is editable, neither right to commercialize it is accepted, except with the consent of the author or authorized distributor. You must purchase this Title from a vendor who's right is given to sell it, other sources of purchase are not accepted, and accountable for an action against. We are happy that you understood, and being guided by these terms as you proceed. Thank you

First Printing: 2017.

ISBN: 978-1-912483-47-1

Publisher: Global Print Digital.
Arlington Row, Bibury, Cirencester GL7 5ND
Gloucester
United Kingdom.
Website: www.homeworkoffer.com
.

Table of Content

Summary 1
Recomendation 18
Background 29
Under Siege: Doda and the Border Districts 41
    Rape and Torture in Doda 49
    Extrajudicial Executions in Doda 52
    Militant Abuses in Doda and other Southern Districts 66
Abuses in the Kashmir Valley 71
    Extrajudicial Executions 73
    Disappearances 80
    Torture 95
Undermining the Judiciary 107
    Detention Practices that Facilitate Abuse 110
    Detentions for Extortion 125
Abuses Involving Counter militant Militias 128
Threats against Human Rights Defenders 141
Attacks on the Press 153
The Ongoing Problem of Impunity 158
Militant Abuses in the Valley 166
The Applicable International Law 170
    Human Rights Law 170
    International Humanitarian Law 171

Summary

The dramatic escalation in May 1999 of cross-border shelling between India and Pakistan, and fighting between Indian troops and militants who have crossed over from Pakistan, have focused international attention on the security implications of the conflict. But the pattern of systematic human rights violations by all parties in Kashmir has been a critical factor in fueling the conflict that is often overlooked. If those violations had been seriously addressed at any time during the last ten years, the risk of a military confrontation between India and Pakistan might have been reduced.

This report documents human rights abuses in Indian-controlled Kashmir by both Indian security forces and Muslim militants, many of them believed to be Pakistani-trained, who have been fighting for independence. Focusing on the border areas in southern Kashmir that have emerged as important new areas of conflict since 1996, it also documents abuses that took place in the Kashmir valley in late 1998, based on extensive interviews with residents and government officials conducted during a mission in October 1998. Our goal is to provide some insight into the nature of the conflict, the way its geographic focus has shifted since 1996, the increasingly communal aspects of the longstanding political and territorial dispute, and measures that all parties to the conflict should take to prevent further abuses. The escalation in fighting has made it all the more urgent that the international community ensure these measures are taken.

The Kashmir conflict not only continues to raise the spectre of war between India and Pakistan, but it also continues to produce serious human rights violations: summary executions, rape, and torture by both sides. In their effort to curb support for pro-independence militants, Indian security forces have resorted to arbitrary arrest and collective punishments of entire neighborhoods, tactics which have only led to further disaffection from India. The militants have kidnapped and killed civil servants and suspected informers. These actions, together with the fact that many of the militants are crossing into India from Pakistan, have reinforced India's determination to eliminate the security threat by any means necessary. Indeed, the Indian air strikes that began in May were in response to the incursion from Pakistan-controlled Kashmir of a large contingent of militant forces into mountainous areas north of Kargil and Dras.

That incursion is part of the same pattern of militant activity documented in this report. Since 1996, as Indian forces have gained the upper hand in the major towns and villages of the Kashmir valley, militant groups have concentrated their efforts on occupying strategic areas along Kashmir's far northern and southern borders, including the districts of Rajouri, Punch, and Doda. In the early years of the conflict, the militants were largely from the Kashmir valley. With support from Pakistan, they were fighting for independence from India and some for accession to Pakistan. Although militant groups in Kashmir continue to draw recruits from among the local population, since 1996 the militant groups in these border areas have been predominantly Pakistani Kashmiris who support the independence struggle, or Pakistanis from elsewhere in the country who have been drawn to the conflict for ideological reasons. The groups often include Afghans and other foreign fighters who have no local base, although they may recruit local Kashmiri men to join them. The fact that a large contingent of these forces have entrenched in the high mountains near the towns of Kargil and Dras on the Indian side of the cease-fire line, known as the Line of Control, represents a major escalation in the conflict.

The reasons for the geographic shift from the Kashmir valley to the border areas lie in the changing military dimensions of the conflict. Indian forces have decimated the ranks of the militant groups operating inside Kashmir. The Jammu and Kashmir Liberation Front, a militant organization that was reputed to command the most popular support among Kashmiris, abandoned the military struggle in 1994. The remaining groups, most of which have close ties to Pakistan, have been largely driven to the more remote mountain areas of Doda and other southern districts from whose rugged terrain they launch attacks on

Indian security forces and local civilians. Between 1997 and mid-1999, these groups have massacred more than 300 civilians. Several of those incidents are documented in this report. Although no organization has claimed responsibility for any of those massacres, two militant groups, Harakat-ul Ansar and Lashgar-i Toiba, are known to operate in the area and both include non-Kashmiris in their ranks. Although so-called foreigners operating in Kashmir outside of the Kargil region number at most a few hundred, they represent a dangerous development in the conflict as they have no accountability to the local population and engage in acts of extreme violence with little regard for the outrage such attacks elicit from Hindu and Muslim Kashmiris alike.

The Indian army has retaliated by conducting cordon-and-search operations in Muslim neighborhoods throughout these districts, detaining young men, assaulting other family members and summarily executing suspected militants. The brutal tactics employed resemble those used in the early 1990s in the Kashmir valley-- indiscriminate shootings and assaults, rape, and arson--that provoked widespread anger among the local population. While such wholesale attacks on civilians have decreased in the valley as Indian forces have consolidated their hold there, they have increased in the southern border districts where they are perceived by the local population as an attempt by Indian forces to punish the Muslim community at large. Aggravating the situation, the army has recruited ex-servicemen, who for historical reasons are almost exclusively Hindu, to serve in Village Defence Committees (VDCs) that assist the army in military operations. In Doda and the border districts, where the population is nearly evenly divided between Hindus and Muslims, there is growing concern that tensions between the two communities might ignite a wider communal conflict.

Elsewhere in Kashmir, most of the militant groups have lost considerable ground militarily, their ranks diminished through infiltration and assassination by "countermilitant" militias made up of former guerrillas and by the government's long policy of summarily executing captured guerrillas. Thus Srinagar and other towns in the valley now seldom see genuine military engagements between militants and state forces. Militant operations in the cities are generally limited to hit-and-run grenade or sniper attacks and assassinations of political leaders, civil servants and suspected informers.

Despite the election in September 1996 of a civilian government in the state of Jammu and Kashmir, and Indian government claims that "normalcy" has returned there, abuses by the army, federal paramilitary forces and a newly constituted police force are rife. Indian forces also continue to arm and train countermilitant militias to assassinate suspected militant activists and intimidate local residents. Although some militant leaders command popular support, extortion and other abuses by the militant groups and their failure to prevail against the Indian forces have left the population embittered. At the same time, ongoing brutality and repression by Indian troops continues to fuel popular discontent and fear. India may have largely crushed its armed opposition in Srinagar and other cities in the Kashmir valley, but it has won little support from the Kashmiris.

As they have gained greater control of the cities, Indian forces and the countermilitants have fostered a climate of repression. Although government troops who no longer fear an ambush are less trigger-happy than was the case in the early 1990s when retaliatory shootings of civilians in crowded urban areas and villages were common, targeted executions continue. Detentions and "disappearances" have left residents fearful of talking to international human rights organizations. Little human rights documentation is done because human rights activists and lawyers have been killed or threatened. Doctors who have treated torture victims have also been threatened and spoke to Human Rights Watch only when assured strict confidentiality.

Custodial killings -- the summary execution of detainees -- remain a central component of the Indian government's counterinsurgency strategy. While the difficulties associated with documentation make it impossible to state accurately the number of such killings, human rights groups in the state and elsewhere in India estimate that such summary executions number in the thousands. In this report,

Human Rights Watch documents nine that occurred in 1998 and one that occurred in 1997. The killings continue because they have the sanction of senior Indian officials who justify them on the grounds that there is no other way to counter a serious "terrorist" threat. Since the insurgency erupted in Kashmir in 1989, there has been no effort on the part of the government to reduce the incidence of custodial killing.

"Disappearances" of detainees also remain a serious problem. Not only has the practice continued, but there has been no accountability for hundreds of cases of "disappearances" that have taken place since 1990. The Kashmir Monitor, a human rights group based in Srinagar, has documented 300 cases of "disappearances" and claims that the actual number is much higher. An association of the parents of the "disappeared," one of the few human rights groups functioning in the state, has been unable to persuade the government to provide information about their missing sons. During its mission, Human Rights Watch documented thirteen cases of "disappearances": two from 1998, nine from 1997, one from 1996 and one from 1995.

The Indian security forces also engage in brutal forms of torture which likewise have the sanction of senior officials. The latter privately justify the practice on the grounds that there is no other way to obtain information from a suspect. In fact, torture is also routinely used to punish suspected militants and their supporters and to extort money from their families. Human Rights Watch documented three cases of torture in this report, one of which took place in October 1998, the other two of which describe a series of detentions in which torture occurred from 1996 until 1998. In one case, two detainees who confessed to having weapons after undergoing severe torture were later berated by an army officer for lying and then released. Human Rights Watch staff also interviewed doctors who had treated former detainees who had been tortured. Methods of torture include severe beatings with truncheons, rolling a heavy log on the legs, hanging the detainee upside down, use of electric shocks, immersion in water while being suspended upside down, and the insertion of an iron rod on which chili paste has been applied into the rectum. Extensive beatings and use of the roller frequently lead to renal damage or failure; being suspended for prolonged periods upside down can lead to nerve damage and paralysis of the limbs.

Hospitals in Srinagar have registered more than 180 patients with torture-induced renal problems since 1994, some one hundred of which were admitted since 1996. These figures only include those cases serious enough to require treatment in the hospital. Of the 180 cases, six died of renal failure. Some of the survivors have suffered permanent damage.

Indian security forces have raped women in Kashmir during search operations, particularly in remote areas outside of major cities and towns. The difficulties inherent in documenting such attacks on women are many. The victims are unlikely to seek medical attention unless their injuries are severe and are reluctant to report their assaults because of the shame and stigma that they may bear as a result. Nonetheless, Human Rights Watch documented one case of rape by the Indian army in Doda and received consistent reports of such abuse from elsewhere in Doda and from the border areas of Punch and Rajouri. Significantly, army authorities have demonstrated some concern about rape and have initiated a number of courts-martial of soldiers for rape. However, many reports of rape, particularly by federal or local police forces, are never investigated.

Prosecutions of security personnel responsible for abuses are rare. The State Human Rights Commission, which is mandated to investigate complaints of human rights violations and make non-binding recommendations to the government, began its work in early 1998 and by November of that year had undertaken investigations in some 200 cases. The commission does not take up cases pending before the High Court. In addition, the commission's work is severely hampered by the fact that it cannot directly investigate abuses carried out by the army or other federal forces. These forces conduct their own investigations, the results of which are not made public. Although government officials claim that disciplinary measures have been taken against some security personnel, criminal prosecutions do not take place.

This report is based on a mission to Indian-controlled Kashmir in October 1998. In the course of that mission Human Rights Watch visited Srinagar, Pampore, Uri, Jammu and Doda. We conducted more than fifty interviews with doctors, lawyers, journalists, human rights activists and other residents of Kashmir. We interviewed leading members of the All-Parties Hurriyat Conference, the political umbrella organization of the militant organizations. Although India does not officially permit international human rights organizations to conduct investigations, Human Rights Watch staff met with representatives of the state government, including Chief Secretary Ashok Jaitley, Justice Kuchay and other members of the State Human Rights Commission, and Superintendent of Police in Doda Munir Khan. We also interviewed leading advocates for the displaced Kashmir Hindus in Jammu, and a local leader of one of the most prominent countermilitant organizations.

Recomendation

Human Rights Watch makes the following recommendations for action to be taken by the government of India, the militant forces in Kashmir, the government of Pakistan, and the international community to address the human rights crisis in Kashmir.

To the Government of India

The government of India should immediately initiate an impartial investigation into reports that the Eighth Rashtriya Rifles Battalion in Doda has been responsible for summary executions, "disappearances," rape, and other assaults on villagers. Other army units and security personnel named in other incidents of abuse should also be investigated and members found responsible for abuse prosecuted and punished.

The State Human Rights Commission should immediately establish branch offices in Doda, Rajouri and Punch to initiate inquiries into allegations of abuse, and provide support to local human rights organizations operating there. The commission should be empowered to investigate even those cases under review by the court.

Village defense committees (VDCs) should not be recruited along communal lines; existing VDCs that are communally based should be disbanded. All such groups should immediately be disarmed unless they are brought within the chain of command of the regular military. Members of VDCs responsible for extrajudicial killings, assaults, and other abuses should be prosecuted. Members of the security forces who have recruited VDC members for forced labor should be prosecuted.

Major Avtar Singh of the 35th Rashtriya Rifles should be apprehended immediately and prosecuted for the March 1996 murder of human rights lawyer and JKLF member Jalil Andrabi.

The Indian government should invite the United Nations Special Rapporteur on Religious Intolerance to Kashmir and, in particular, to the Doda region to look into reports that abuses by militant groups and by the Indian army and village defense committees are contributing to a rise in communal tension. It should also permit the relevant United Nations special rapporteurs and working groups to conduct investigations.

The government of India should ensure that all reports of extrajudicial executions, "disappearances," deaths in custody, torture, and rape by security forces and unofficial paramilitary forces in Kashmir are investigated promptly by a judicial authority empowered to subpoena security force officers and official registers and other documents. Security personnel, including police, army, and paramilitary, responsible for these abuses should be prosecuted in civilian courts. Only with such trials and appropriate punishments will these forces receive the clear, unequivocal message that human rights violations are not condoned by their superiors. Those found guilty of abuse should be punished regardless of rank. The punishments should be at least as severe as those specified under civilian law. The results of these investigations and the punishments should be made public as a means of giving the people of Kashmir a reason to believe in the government's commitment to justice and the rule of law. Orders should be given immediately that police are to register all reports of abuse; anyone in the security forces found to have issued contrary instructions and any member of the police who has refused to register cases should be disciplined to the full extent of the law.

The government of India should disarm and disband all state-sponsored militias not established and regulated by law and prosecute members of such groups who have been responsible for extrajudicial killings, "disappearances," assaults, and other abuses. The government of India should establish a civilian review board to oversee any rehabilitation program for surrendered militants. This review board should have access to records on surrendered weapons and should review vocational training programs to ensure that the former militants are not compelled to serve in state paramilitary forces not established and regulated by law, or induced to take part in security operations that violate international human rights and humanitarian law.

Although the government of India has promised since 1993 to establish a centralized register of detainees accessible to lawyers and family members, this has never happened. In addition, security personnel continue to defy court orders to produce detainees in court. Both of these factors have increased the likelihood of "disappearances." The government of India should take stern and swift action against all officers who have obstructed or ignored judicial orders to produce detainees. All places of detention should be made known to the court and be subject to regular inspection by a magistrate. In addition, the security agencies should require that arresting officers provide signed receipts for all detainees to family members, village elders, or persons of similar status. The receipt would be retrieved when the person is released.

In previous reports, Human Rights Watch has urged the government of India to provide police training, perhaps after consultation with international experts, on gathering adequate evidence for rape prosecutions. Explicit prohibitions against rape should be included in training for all enlisted men and officers in the police, paramilitary forces, and military as a way of sending a clear signal that rape is not tolerated by the state. Medical workers who have examined and treated rape victims should be protected from abuse. Medical facilities, including private licensed physicians, should be encouraged to give testimony and introduce physical evidence in court with regard to rape and other forms of sexual and physical abuse.

State authorities and the headquarters of the army and paramilitary operations in Kashmir should issue public statements affirming the security of human rights defenders. The statements should include explicit guarantees for the security of human rights monitors to investigate incidents of abuse, record the statements of witnesses, publicize their reports, and petition the courts.

To the Militant Organizations

Militant groups should immediately stop all attacks on civilians, including kidnappings and assassinations. Militant groups should abide by human rights norms and the provisions of Common Article 3 of the Geneva Conventions which prohibit hostage-taking, cruel, inhuman, and degrading treatment, and executions.

Militant groups should desist from using anti-personnel landmines.

To the Government of Pakistan

The government of Pakistan should end all support for abusive militant organizations in Kashmir. It should not provide indiscriminate weapons, such as landmines, to such groups.

To the United Nations

The General Assembly should condemn abuses by both Indian security forces and militants in Kashmir and urge India to permit relevant U.N. working groups and special rapporteurs to visit Kashmir.

The High Commissioner on Human Rights should visit Kashmir and conduct an investigation into abuses by all parties to the conflict. Her findings and recommendations should be reported to the Security Council and the General Assembly and should be made publicly available.

To the International Community

France, Germany, Russia, the U.K., the U.S., and India's other trading partners should suspend all military aid and sales and all programs of military cooperation with India, including joint exercises, until India provides greater accountability on cases of "disappearances," torture, and summary killings by its forces in Kashmir and disarms all state-sponsored paramilitary groups operating in Kashmir.

At the annual World Bank-sponsored donors meeting on India, participant countries should publicly state that continued economic support for India should not been seen as support for the Indian government's human rights policies. In the statement, and in private and public meetings with Indian government officials, members of the donor group should raise concerns about deteriorating conditions in Doda and other border districts and press India to allow greater access to these areas and other parts of Kashmir to international organizations. They should press India to invite the U.N. special rapporteurs and the working groups to visit Kashmir. They should also raise concerns about attacks on human rights defenders in Kashmir.

The diplomatic staff of India's allies and trading partners should make a point of visiting areas of the state outside the Kashmir valley, particularly Doda, Rajouri and Punch, and ensure that their reports reflect current human rights conditions in these areas.

The international community should condemn Pakistan's support for abusive militant groups operating in Kashmir and make any future arms sales or military cooperation agreements contingent on an end to Pakistan's support for abusive militant groups.

Background

Kashmir has been at the heart of a territorial dispute between India and Pakistan since the two nations gained their independence in 1947. Both claim Kashmir. In 1948 the then-ruler of the princely state of Jammu and Kashmir, Maharaja Hari Singh, who was holding out for independence, acceded to India on condition that the state retain autonomy in all matters except defense, currency and foreign affairs. The accession was provoked by the invasion of Pakistani raiders and an uprising of villagers in the western part of the state. Fighting between India and Pakistan ended with U.N. intervention; since 1948 the cease-fire line has been monitored by the U.N. Military Observer Group on India and Pakistan (UNMOGIP). The far northern and western areas of the state are under Pakistan's control; the Kashmir valley, Jammu, and Ladakh are under India's control. U.N. resolutions calling for a plebiscite to determine the final status of the territory have been rejected by India, which claims that because Kashmiris have voted in national elections in India, there is no need for a plebiscite. Pakistan maintains that a plebiscite should be held. Several of the militant groups in Kashmir have also called for a plebiscite but argue that an independent Kashmir should be an option. On July 2, 1972, India and Pakistan signed the Simla Accord, under which both countries agreed to respect the cease-fire line, known as the Line of Control, and to resolve differences over Kashmir "by peaceful means" through negotiation. The Simla Accord left the "final settlement" of the Kashmir question to be resolved at an unspecified future date.

Since then, the Simla Accord has been the touchstone of all bilateral discussions of the Kashmir issue, even though the accord itself left the issue unresolved.

India's efforts to manipulate elections in Kashmir and suppress dissent have marked Kashmir's history since 1948, but it was not until 1986 that discontent within the state found wider popular support. In that year the state's ruling National Conference (NC) party, widely accused of corruption, struck a deal with India's Congress Party administration that many in Kashmir saw as a betrayal of Kashmir's autonomy. A new party, the Muslim United Front (MUF), attracted the support of a broad range of Kashmiris, including pro-independence activists, disenchanted Kashmiri youth and the pro-Pakistan Jama'at-i Islami, an Islamic political organization, and appeared poised to do well in state elections in 1987. Blatant rigging assured a National Conference victory, which was followed by the arrests of hundreds of MUF leaders and supporters. In the aftermath, young MUF supporters swelled the ranks of agrowing number of militant groups who increasingly crossed over to Pakistan for arms and training. The major militant organizations were divided between those advocating an independent Kashmir and those supporting accession to Pakistan. In the late 1980s, the groups began assassinating NC leaders and engaging in other acts of violence. Some groups also targeted Hindu families, and a slow exodus of Hindus from the valley began.

After the elections, militants of the JKLF and other groups stepped up their attacks on the government, detonating bombs at government buildings, buses, and the houses of present and former state officials, and enforcing a state-wide boycott of the November 1989 national parliamentary elections. One month later, JKLF militants abducted the daughter of Home Minister

Mufti Mohammad Sayeed, then freed her when the government gave in to demands for the release of five detained militants. That event, together with a surge in popular protest against the state and central governments, led the central government to launch a massive crackdown on the militants.

On January 19, 1990, the central government imposed direct rule on the state. From the outset, the Indian government's campaign against the militants was marked by widespread human rights violations, including the shooting of unarmed demonstrators, civilian massacres, and summary executions of detainees. Militant groups stepped up their attacks, murdering and threatening Hindu residents, carrying out kidnappings and assassinations of government officials, civil servants, and suspected informers, and engaging in sabotage and bombings. With the encouragement and assistance of the government, some 100,000 Hindu Kashmiris, known as "Pandits," fled the valley. By May 1990, rising tension between Pakistan and India following the escalation of the conflict in Kashmir raised fears of another war between the two countries.

In late 1993, the All Parties Hurriyat Conference (APHC), an umbrella organization of the leaders of all the political and militant organizations fighting for independence, was founded to act as the political voice of the independence movement. However, rivalries within the APHC have limited its effectiveness. Charges of corruption have also tainted some APHC leaders.[1]

In the mid-1990s, Indian security forces began arming and training local auxiliary forces made up of surrendered or captured militants to assist in counterinsurgency operations. These state-sponsored paramilitary groups have committed serious human rights abuses, and human rights defenders and journalists have been among the principal victims.

In May 1996, parliamentary elections were held in the state for the first time since 1989. Militant leaders called for a boycott, however, and there were widespread reports that security forces had forced some voters to go to the polls. During state assembly elections in September of that year as well, residents-particularly those living in Srinagar and other cities-also complained that the security forces had tried to counter a militant boycott by forcing some people to go to the polls. However, a large number appeared to have voted voluntarily. Following the election, the National Conference party formed the first state government since 1990. Farooq Abdullah, who together with leaders from the Congress Party had been responsible for rigging state elections in 1987, again became chief minister.

On May 11 and 13, 1998, India tested five nuclear devices, and three weeks later, Pakistan responded in kind. The tests ignited a firestorm of criticism around the world and triggered sanctions by both countries' donors and trading partners. In the months following the tests, an upsurge in shelling and shooting by Indian and Pakistani troops stationed along the cease-fire line in Kashmir left over one hundred civilians dead. Following a the Indian prime minister's historic bus trip from New Delhi to the Pakistan border in February 1999, the prime ministers of both countries signed the Lahore Declaration in which they vowed, among other things, to renew talks on Kashmir and to alert each other of further arms tests. Following such a warning, on April 11,1999, India test-fired its long-range Agni missile, and on April 14 and 15, Pakistan did the same with its long-range Gauri and medium-range Shaheenmissiles. India conducted another ballistic missile test on April 16; the exchange again raised international concern about the prospects for an arms race on the subcontinent.

Rising tensions in the region have made clear that both India and Pakistan have legitimate security concerns related to Kashmir. But these concerns justify neither the abuses committed by Indian military and paramilitary forces nor Pakistan's support for fighters who have also committed serious human rights violations.

Parties to the Conflict

As of 1999, the major militant organizations fighting in Kashmir included the Hizb-ul Mujahidin, Harakat-ul Ansar and Lashgar-i Toiba. The latter two, in particular, are reported to include a large number of non-Kashmiris. Most of these groups support accession to Pakistan. The Jammu and Kashmir Liberation Front (JKLF), the organization that spearheaded the movement for an independent Kashmir, declared a cease-fire in 1994. All groups have reportedly received arms and training from Pakistan. The weapons they have used include AK-47 and AK-56 assault rifles, light machine guns, revolvers, and landmines. The militants are also reported to have sophisticated night-vision and wireless communication equipment. Officially, the Pakistani government has denied involvement in arming and training Kashmiri militants, but the claim is generally not considered credible.

Central government forces operating in Kashmir include the Indian Army and India's federal security forces, the Central Reserve Police Force (CRPF), and the Border Security Force (BSF). The army's role in the conflict expanded in 1993 with the introduction of the Rashtriya Rifles, an elite army unit created specifically for counterinsurgency operations in Kashmir. The Rashtriya Rifles have been the main force in charge of counterinsurgency operations in Doda, Rajouri and Punch. As of June 1999, some 400,000 army troops and other federal security forces were deployed in the valley, including those positioned along the Line of Control.

In May 1999 India deployed thousands of additional troops to the Kargil region. The local Jammu and Kashmir policemen are generally not involved in counterinsurgency operations, largely because they are believed to be sympathetic to the insurgency. However, in 1995 the Special Task Force (STF) and the Special Operations Group (SOG), counterinsurgency divisions of the Jammu and Kashmir Police made up of non-Muslim non-Kashmiri recruits, including some former militants, were formed apparently to create the impression that the counterinsurgency effort had local support. These police forces frequently operate jointly with the Rashtriya Rifles.

Since at least early 1995 Indian security forces have armed and trained local auxiliary forces made up of surrendered or captured militants to assist in counterinsurgency operations. These forces, who function outside of the normal command structure of the Indian army and other security forces, nevertheless are considered state agents under international law. These groups participate in joint patrols, receive and carry out orders given by security officers, and operate in full view of army and security force bunkers and camps. Some members of these groups are even housed in military compounds. They include Ikhwan-ul Muslimoon and Muslim Mujahidin.

Under Siege: Doda and the Border Districts

Rajouri, Punch, and Doda lie between Jammu and the Kashmir valley in the rugged foothills south of the Pir Panjal mountain range. The area is poorly developed, with minimal road links and communications. Its population is roughly divided between Hindus and Muslims and includes a variety of linguistic groups other than Kashmiris.

Although the mountain passes along the border areas of Rajouri and Punch have long been used as transit areas for militant groups crossing over from Pakistan, they did not become a focal point of militant operations until after 1995, when the Indian counterinsurgency forces had driven many of the militant groups from their strongholds in the Kashmir valley. The geographic shift also reflected a shift in the tactics and character of the militant groups who began to operate in the area. Having suffered a political schism, and having lost a large number of senior leaders who were captured and then apparently executed in late 1994, the JKLF declared an end to its military operations in 1994. The principal groups engaged in armed conflict with Indian forces after that point were the Hizb-ul Mujahidin and a number of small groups, including Harakat-ul Ansar and Lashgar-i Toiba. All are pro-Pakistani; the latter two are believed to include members who are Pakistani and Afghan.

Munir Khan, superintendent of police in Doda, told Human Rights Watch that he estimated that there were 700-800 militants in the area. Because of the rough terrain, the militants have an advantage over the security forces and can launch attacks on remote areas that are difficult for the police and army to reach. He blamed the militants for inflaming communal tensions in the region.

The militants are trying to communalize the issue... There is an escalation, a worsening cycle. I have seen it in Baramula where militants undertake a certain action and the security forces fight back. But contrary to the militants, we are accountable: We must answer to our superior officers ... and we face inquiries, departmental elections, and legal action. The population is 48 percent Hindu and 52 percent Muslim. Any action has a reaction. Even Muslims are killed by the militants-95 percent of the Muslims do not voluntarily support the militants. There are two ways of pressure: money, and outright coercion. Money matters. The local militants want to surrender. This month [October 1998], eleven did and four were killed. The mercenaries put pressure on the people via threats. The security forces can't protect everyone at all times. As for the actions by the security forces, mistakes do happen, but we repent, and it is not willful. And even if it is not intentional, we have to answer to many forums. This is a proxy war. Collateral damage is much higher in this type of war. Things happen in the heat of the moment.

Beginning in 1995, militant groups began to systematically attack Hindu villagers in the area. Although militant groups had targeted Hindu communities and individuals previously, these new and apparently indiscriminate attacks were marked by a viciousness that had not previously been seen in the conflict. Nineteen-ninety-eight was a particularly bad year; more than 200 civilians were killed in attacks by these groups. In 1999, militant groups used the occasion of the historic summit between the prime ministers of India and Pakistan on February 20 to massacre twenty Hindu civilians in three separate attacks in Kashmir.

The Indian government blamed "foreign" militants for those attacks and has continued to argue that the conflict in Kashmir has largely become a fight between these foreign forces-which it claims number in the hundreds-and its own troops. At the same time, government forces have targeted local Muslim villagers whom they have accused of providing support for the militants. In fact, some of the attacks appear to have been carried out by local groups or those that have local members. In response to the attacks, the government has deployed the RashtriyaRifles to conduct extensive combing operations in the mountains and cordon-and-search operations in the villages in search of the militants and their suspected supporters.

The brutality exhibited by the army during these operations appears designed to punish local villagers suspected of supporting the militants and as such, is reminiscent of the behavior of Indian forces in the Kashmir valley in the early 1990s: whole neighborhoods and villages have been surrounded, the residents beaten and subjected to other abuse, and property damaged or destroyed. Those detained most frequently are young men who because of their age or appearance are suspected of being militants; torture of detainees is routine. There are consistent reports that some Indian troops have raped women in these villages. Indian forces have also summarily executed suspected militants; an unknown number of detainees has disappeared following arrest. Witnesses and survivors have named one army unit in particular as being responsible for rape, torture, and extrajudicial execution: the Eighth Rashtriya Rifles.

Since at least 1996, the security forces-principally the Indian Army-have armed local Village Defence Committees (VDCs) in Doda, Udhampur, and the border districts to assist in security operations. The basis for recruitment is previous military service; for historical reasons, the only men with military experience are Hindu. Most Muslim men who served in the military at the time of independence left after partition for Pakistan. Thus, the only men who have previous military service are Hindu, with the result that the VDCs have become a communally based militia sponsored and armed by the Indian Army but operating outside of its chain of command. Members of the VDCs have accompanied army soldiers during cordon-and-search operations in Muslim villages and neighborhoods. They have been responsible for serious abuses, including extrajudicial executions and assaults. Human Rights Watch interviewed one Muslim member of a VDC who had been ordered to do manual labor for the army:

The security forces and the militants used to come to our village and beat us. But after I set up the VDC, the situation got worse, not better. The army has told me that I have a choice either to work for them or join the militants. The *muezzin*[prayer-caller] was told not to call for prayers from the mosque. Muslims have been made a target. Our village is half Muslim, half Hindu. Our job was to guard the village. But the army has asked us to do construction work for them. I refused, and then they beat me. This happened yesterday.

Human Rights Watch staff observed recent bruises on the man's body.

Because of the relative inaccessibility of many of the villages of these districts, there is little documentation of human rights abuses. Lawyers and journalists from the valley seldom visit the area. One local human rights organization, the Forum for Human Rights and Communal Harmony, has documented incidents of abuse, but unlike in Srinagar, there are few local lawyers available to take up cases.

Rape and Torture in Doda

Indian forces and paramilitary militias working with them have been responsible for rape throughout the conflict. Although the Indian government has prosecuted and punished a number of security personnel for rape, many cases are never investigated. Reports of rape from Doda and other border areas have increased since the crackdown in these areas began in 1997.

The case of S. illustrates the army's practice of assaulting villagers in punishment because they believe they have supported the militants, or as a means of terrorizing them so that they will not do so. S. about fifty, a resident of Ludna, Doda, told Human Rights Watch that on October 5, 1998, the Eighth Rashtriya Rifles came to her house and took her, her husband and her eight-month-old grandson to their base in the village of Charote, some fifteen kilometers away. There they were separated. She said:

They began beating me. They said that we had been feeding the militants. They used electric shocks on my feet. I was raped. They stripped off my clothes and said they would kill me. There were many soldiers and a captain. The captain raped me, keeping everyone else outside. He told me: "You are Muslims, and you will all be treated like this." He was a Hindu, but he told me that he was a Muslim, and that his name was

Shahnawaz. He forced me to confess that I had been feeding the militants. This happened on the first night. I was there for fifteen days. Then we were released.

Ten days after their arrest, while the family was still in Charote, S.'s daughter, daughter-in-law and son were arrested and taken to another army base in Gundna village, where they were held for two days before being released.

When the family returned to their home they discovered that all of their belongings had been taken, including Rs. 10,000 [U.S.$ 250] and jewelry. At the time that Human Rights Watch interviewed S., she had not yet filed a police report but had received medical treatment from a local practitioner. She stated that she was still in pain.

Residents of Marmal, Doda, told Human Rights Watch that in early October 1998 the army cordoned off some twenty villages in the area for fifteen days and during that time took some of the local women to the army camp. Although the women did not talk about what had happened to them, from their behavior the other residents believed that a number of them had been raped.

They are looking for the militants. But they are unable to find any. So they harass the local population .... Our womenfolk are taken into the army camp, all separately. They round up the women, then take two or three in the evening. They come back after two or three days. They are very shy then, and don't want to talk about what has happened to them. The army has pressured them not to speak about what happened.

Extrajudicial Executions in Doda

Since the conflict began in 1989, Indian forces in Kashmir have routinely and systematically detained and executed men suspected of being members or supporters of armed militant groups. There are no known figures for the number of such killings, but in the decade since the conflict began, they number at least several thousand. In the early years of the conflict, human rights activists attempted to compile statistics on the detentions and killings, but their work was generally limited to the larger towns and cities. By 1994, most human rights documentation ceased after several prominent human rights defenders were killed and others were threatened. Since then, a few human rights lawyers have continued to compile statistics on the killings. Though incomplete, their documentation indicates that there has been no change in the government's policy or practice in this regard. "Custodial killings," as they are known in Kashmir, continue to be a hallmark of the government's counterinsurgency operations.

Human Rights Watch investigated ten cases of extrajudicial execution that had occurred between 1997 and 1998. Seven of the incidents took place in the Doda region; the others took place in or near Srinagar. We were not able to investigate reports of extrajudicial killings from other parts of the valley. Other organizations have done so, however. In its 1998 report, the South Asia Human Rights Documentation Center documented fourteen incidents of summary execution and deaths resulting from torture that occurred in 1997 and 1998. The U.S. State Department noted in its 1999 human rights report that

Although well-documented evidence to corroborate cases and quantify trends is lacking, most observers believe that the number of killings attributed to regular Indian forces showed no improvement from the previous year. According to press reports and anecdotal accounts, those killed typically had been detained by security forces, and their bodies, bearing multiple bullet wounds and often marks of torture, were returned to relatives or were otherwise discovered the same day or a few days later.

Reprisal killings of civilians and the routine use of lethal force on a large scale against peaceful demonstrators have declined since 1993 when a number of such incidents prompted international criticism of India's Kashmir policy. However, on January 30, 1998, in one of the deadliest incidents of its kind in years, army soldiers fatally shot at least nine villagers during a search operation in the town of Qadrana in Doda district after some of the villagers began throwing stones at the troops in protest over the arrest of a number of village men.

Security legislation authorizes the security forces to shoot to kill and to destroy civilian property. Under these laws, the security forces are protected from prosecution for human rights violations. House demolitions are carried out under the Special Powers Act, and usually without warning.

Ghulam Qadir Wani

The Eighth Rashtriya Rifles were apparently responsible for the extrajudicial execution of Ghulam Qadir Wani, a resident of Chatta, Doda, who had filed a complaint with local police against the army unit after soldiers from the unit shot and killed a woman in the village and injured Wani's son.

N., a resident of Chatta, a village about twenty kilometers from Doda, told Human Rights Watch that at about 5:45 a.m. on October 21, 1998, when he and other family members were at home, Ghulam Qadir Wani, went upstairs to the roof of the house to pray.

At that time the Eighth Rashtriya Rifles came to the house and encircled it. N. stated:

[Wani] told all of us to stay inside. Some soldiers went up the stairs; others came inside and kept us there. Then we heard shots upstairs. But we were not allowed to go there; we were pushed and beaten. At 9:00 a.m we were allowed to go outside but not upstairs. The army stayed in the house until 2:00 p.m. Then the army called the police, and they came. They went upstairs, and so did I and some soldiers. There I saw [Wani's] body with a cartridge belt next to him and a pistol. These were not his, but must have been placed there. Then the army left, telling the people in the village that they would do the same to the rest of them.

Another villager, P., stated that when Wani's death was announced on the radio, the government claimed that he was a militant and a leader of the Hizb-ul Mujahedin. However, N. told Human Rights Watch that several months before he was killed, Wani had testified against soldiers from the same unit who had killed a woman named Rafiqa, the wife of Mohamed Sharif Lone, on June 27, 1998, and injured Wani's son, Mohammed Ashfaq. Both Wani and his son were detained at an army camp for three days after the incident. Mohammad Ashfaq was accused of being a militant but was then released. Afterwards, both men came to Doda and filed a First Information Report (FIR), the starting point for a criminal investigation, in Rafiqa's death (FIR 83/98).

A neighbor of Wani's, J., stated that the day before Wani was killed, the soldiers told him that they had orders to kill three men in the village: Wani, J., and another man named Gani Darzi, a tailor. J. stated that when he filed a complaint with the police about the threat, the police would not register a case against the army unit. J. stated that he had been detained by the Eighth Rashtriya Rifles unit a number of times and tortured with electric shock. He said that he believed they had singled him out because he had a beard and was very religious. The family lodged a complaint in Wani's death at the police station in Doda, FIR number 148/98.

Imam Din Bhat

On July 24, 1998, Imam-ud-din Bhat, thirty-five, was arrested by the army in the village of Thakrai near Kistwar, about twenty-five kilometers northeast of Doda. His father, Ahmedou Bhat, told Human Rights Watch that when he learned that his son had been arrested, he went to look for him and followed the army as they moved.

They threatened me, saying that I should leave. I went to Kishtwar and stayed there for three days. Then I learned that the army had killed two persons they had previously arrested, and that they had buried them. We lodged a complaint with the police and then went to the burial site with the police and a doctor. There my son and Abdul Rashid, the son of Juma Bakarwal, were exhumed.

Abdul Rashid was twenty-four. According to a statement by Imam-ud-din Bhat's wife, her husband had traveled to the village with Rashid to buy some sheep. On July 28, four days after their arrest, sixteen Hindu civilians were killed in an attack by a militant group in Thakrai and Sarwan. After Bhat and Rashid were killed, the army claimed that the "foreign militants" responsible for the massacre had been killed. In an article published on July 31, the Kashmir Times reported that

[r]esentment prevailed amongst people in Kistwar over failure of [the state] administration to disclose the names of militants killed in an encounter ... after the killings. They alleged that security forces had killed two civilians in a fake encounter and painted them as militants. They identified the civilians as Imam Din ... and Abdul Rashid... They were reported to be missing from their villages.

The bodies were exhumed on August 6. Human Rights Watch obtained a copy of the autopsy report, completed on August 6, which stated that Imam Din and Abdul Rashid died of gunshot wounds. Citing testimony from local witnesses, the autopsy report stated that the burial took place on July 29, 1998.

Saleema Bhat, Mohamed Husein Bhat, Sakeena Bhat and Shabeena Bhat

M., thirty-three, a resident of Kotal, Doda, described the killing of four members of a family by a joint force of the army and VDC on July 25, 1998:

At about 2:00 a.m., four members of a family were killed by seven gunmen in military uniforms. I was there when it happened. I could not see in the dark exactly who they were, but they were a mix of army and VDC. That's the routine; they always come to the village together. They have been coming for about two years, sometimes once a week, sometimes twice. The VDCs also wear uniforms but they have different weapons: the army has the new ones, and the VDC have the old ones.

As with the case of Imam-ud-din Bhat above, the incident followed a massacre of Hindu villagers that had occurred in the villages of Thakrai and Sarwan on July 24. Bhat stated that the security forces were looking for a militant whom they believed may have been involved in the killings.

There were fifteen in the house. They started beating everyone. I hid in a nearby field. Shortly afterwards I heard gunshots and I heard the children screaming, wailing over the deaths. Then the military men left. I went to the house when it became light, and other villagers came to the house as well, as did the police. What I saw was the dead bodies of Saleema, Mohamed Husein, his wife, Sakeena, and their daughter, Shabeena.

Except for the witness himself, all the survivors were children. The family filed a complaint with the police.

Human Rights Watch obtained a copy of the autopsy report which stated that all four died of multiple gunshot wounds. Saleema was thirty; Mohamed Husein was forty-five; his wife, Sakeena, was thirty-five; and their daughter, Shabeena, was eighteen. Saleema's husband filed an FIR with the police.

Mohamed Ashraf

J. told Human Rights Watch that on October 22, 1998, Mohamed Ashraf, along with seven other men, was arrested by the Eighth Rashtriya Rifles. On October 27 he received a message from the army that he could go to thearmy camp at Charote to collect the body. The family refused to go to the camp and later collected the body from the local police. According to the local human rights organization, the Forum for Human Rights and Communal Harmony, Ashraf died as a result of torture. Ashraf was the only one of the eight men arrested who was killed. At the time of the Human Rights Watch interview, the family was in Doda to file a complaint with the police.

"Disappearance" of Mohammad Saleem Zargar

Human Rights Watch obtained information about the "disappearance" of Mohammad Saleem Zargar, son of Ghulam Mohammad Zargar, resident of Doda, who was arrested from his home by Maj. Bhakar Singh and Havaldar [an officer below a major] Jagdish of the 10th Rashtriya Rifles on September 14, 1995. The soldiers first approached Mohammad Saleem Zargar, a contractor, to purchase cement. When they were told that there was none available, they left after first inquiring from a servant the names of all the family members. The soldiers returned that night and asked Mohammad Saleem to accompany them to show them the way to Bhagwah, another village. As it was dark, he refused to do so. The soldiers then became angry and, after beating several family members, forced Mohammad Saleem Zargar into a vehicle and left.

That night the family reported the incident to the army unit and was told that Mohammad Saleem would be released within two hours. The next morning at 8:00 a.m., a group of soldiers from the army unit came to the house and inquired about the incident. The family approached other authorities, including the army brigadier, but were given no information on Mohammad Saleem's whereabouts.

Militant Abuses in Doda and other Southern Districts

Attacks by militant groups on civilians in the Doda district escalated sharply in 1998. The attacks appear to have been motivated both by the militants' intention to drive Hindu residents from the area and to demonstrate to the Indian forces in Kashmir that despite the crackdown in the valley, they could continue to strike at will. In addition to these attacks, militant groups have laid landmines along roads used for civilian traffic. On July 14, 1998, Indian forces claimed to have defused a landmine planted along a route used by Hindus during an annual pilgrimage. According to a report by the British Broadcasting Corporation (BBC), the militant group, Harkat-ul Mujahideen, claimed to have planted the device and had warned Hindus not to make the journey.

On June 19, 1998, twenty-five Hindu residents of Korra, a small village in Doda district, were killed by militant forces as they returned from a wedding in the village of Champnagri. Janak Raj, twenty-five, described the incident to Human Rights Watch:

After the wedding we went up to the roadside to wait for the bus by which we would return to our village. There were two wedding parties waiting there, and the men were standing separately from the women and children. We had been waiting for about fifteen minutes when suddenly five armed men showed up. At first we though they were soldiers. They were wearing uniforms [an apparent ruse], and they asked us, the men, for our ID cards. They were speaking in a Hindustani [Urdu] language. We showed them our cards. They lined us up in two lines. Then they told us to hand them over everything we had. The moment we started opening our bags, they opened fire at us with their rifles. I was standing in the line, and the person next to me was hit and toppled against and over me. This is how I was saved. I was not hit, and lay below my friend. I remained conscious, and stayed down for fifteen minutes. I don't know what happened to the armed men.Then a boy of about ten started crying: "What happened? What happened?" So I got up. I don't know where he was or wherethe women were. There was nobody there. Everybody had run away. There is a village some three kilometers nearby, Ganika. So I went there. A bit up from the road from there, there is an army picket. First the police came, and ther the army. A total of twenty-five men were killed.

No group claimed responsibility for the attack. However, according to Superintendent of Police Munir Khan, the leader of the group responsible was a militant called Siraj Din, code name Mansour, of the Harakat-ul Ansar. He was a local from the village of Kotal. At the time of the interview he had been arrested and was in prison in Jammu.

The incident was one of a series of such attacks that occurred in 1998. On April 19, 1998, unidentified gunmen killed twenty-seven members of several Hindu families, including eleven children, in the village of Prankote, in Udhampur. The attackers also set fire to a number of houses. According to a report in the *Washington Post*, the attackers used scythes and axes to carry out the killings. One teenaged girl was also raped and then set on fire. She later died from her burns.

On July 28, 1998 , at least sixteen Hindu villagers were killed in two separate attacks in the villages of Thakrai and Sarwan in Doda district. Most were killed in their homes by gunmen who opened fire with automatic weapons. On August 1, 1998, at least four Hindus were killed and one injured when militants attacked a village in Udhampur district.

Abuses in the Kashmir Valley

The Kashmir valley, which includes all of the major towns and villages along the Jhelum river to the north of Srinagar to Handwara and south to Anantnag, has been at the center of the insurgency since 1989. It is predominantly Muslim and Kashmiri-speaking. Most of the major militant groups have political representation through the All-Parties Hurriyat Conference, based in Srinagar. Many of the groups continue to command popular support in Srinagar and throughout the valley. However, their military capabilities have been severely undermined by the Indian government's use of countermilitant militias made up of former guerrillas who have infiltrated the militant groups and have assassinated and informed on their former colleagues. As a result, military engagements between militant and Indian government forces generally take place in more remote areas outside of the towns and villages of the valley, and the groups' presence in the urban areas has been reduced.

Prominent militant leaders taken into custody were among those executed. In an incident that sparked protests throughout Kashmir, on April 20, 1998, security forces from the Special Operations Group (SOG), a police counterinsurgency unit, detained S. Hamid, chairman of one of the factions of the Jammu and Kashmir People'sLeague. The next day the authorities claimed he had been killed in a shootout. Relatives who witnessed the arrest, however, stated that he was dragged out to the porch of his house and shot.

Many detentions carried out by Indian security forces in Kashmir occur after "crackdowns"-cordon-and-search operations during which all the men of a neighborhood or village are called to assemble for an identification parade in front of hooded informers. Those whom the informers point out are taken away for torture and interrogation, and some are simply taken away and shot. In those cases, officials in Kashmir routinely claim that the detainee was killed in an "encounter" with the security forces, or was shot trying to escape.

Extrajudicial Executions

Ghulam Hassan Ganie

At about midnight on September 14-15, 1998, Ghulam Hassan Ganie, twenty-eight, was arrested in his house in Patel Bagh, Pampore, by a combined force of army and Special Task Force. Two other residents of the area, Abderrashid Bhat and Mohamed Jabbar Wani, were also arrested. L., who witnessed the arrest, told Human Rights Watch that the next day, September 15, the relatives went to the local police station of Pampore to report the arrests. In the evening, the state police administration publicly announced the arrest of the three men as suspected militants.

Early on Monday, September 16, a rumor spread in the village that one of the detainees had been killed during an encounter and that his body could be recovered from the Srinagar police station, eighteen kilometers away. At 1:00 p.m. that day, the police of Shergali, the main local police station of Civil Lines, Srinagar, told the family that Ganie's body had been found near the station. The Shregali police handed the body over to the Pampore police, who handed it over to the family.

L., who saw the body, stated that Ganie had a bloody scar on the right cheek and a depressed chest. There were no other marks, and no bullet wounds. In the official police bulletin of that evening, nothing was said about the case.

Ganie had previously been arrested in 1996 because of his involvement with a militant group, and was jailed for two years. He was released in April 1998.

On September 16-17, the people in the village protested the arrests and killing, and because the village is located on the main highway, they managed to block traffic. Villagers stated that as a result of the public pressure, the two other men were released at 7:00 p.m. on September 17 by the Jammu and Kashmir Light Infantry, an army unit whose headquarters is situated behind the Shergali police station. According to L., the two men have been too frightened to talk about the incident. At the time of Human Rights Watch interview, the family had received no explanation about Ganie's killing.

Ali Mohamed Bhatt

Ali Mohamed Bhatt was arrested in his home in Shoragrera Mohalla, Nawab Bazar, Srinagar on August 8, 1998 and executed that night. Aisha Bhatt, his wife, told Human Rights Watch that two men who were staying in the house at the time were also arrested and killed; the witness did not know their names. At 11:30 p.m. on August 8, a police team headed by the station house officer (SHO) of the police station of Mahraj Gunj, Srinagar, raided the house. Bhatt and the two men were taken away. Aisha Bhatt and their three children were also taken that night andheld in the police station for three days. When she was released she learned that her husband and the two other men were dead and that the bodies of the three men had been handed over to relatives for burial on the evening of August 9. After the killings, the Jammu and Kashmir police chief issued a press statement announcing that all three men had been killed in an encounter. Because the authorities claim that the house had been used by militants, Aisha Bhatt was unable to reclaim possession of it.

Mohamed Amin

W., a resident of Badran, Badgam, described the summary execution of Mohamed Amin. Amin had been a member of the Hizb-ul Mujahedin since 1993. In the fall of 1995 he was arrested by the army in Tangmarg, Baramula. He was held at the army camp for five days, and then they moved him to Zainakoot army camp on the outskirts of Srinagar. His family was allowed to meet him there about fifteen days after this arrest. He had been badly beaten and and been given electric shocks. He had been given the roller treatment and had been forced to drink his own urine. He was released after being held for one month. Over the next year, Amin was arrested and tortured eight times; each time he was detained in the morning and released in the evening. On February 20, 1997 he was called to the army camp and detained there but was released the same day. W. described what happened next:

The next day, first a civilian man came to see whether Amin was home. After they were assured that he was, an army unit headed by Major Shekawar came at 9:30 p.m. and took him to Aripathen camp, which is the military camp of our area. At midnight they returned with him and told him to show them where the weapons were buried. But there were no weapons, so they returned to the camp. At 2:00 a.m. they came back again, but he still did not produce any weapons, so then they took his brother, Abdurrashid, and beat him with their guns and sticks and kicked him with their boots. Then they took Mohamed Amin to another house in the village and started beating him there.

The army stayed in the village till noon the next day and then went back to the army camp with Amin. The next morning, February 23, at 7:00 a.m., residents of the village found Amin's body tied to a tree on the outskirts of the village. W. stated:

I immediately went there. His body was riddled with bullets. The bone of his forehead protruded, one eye was out, all the fingers of his left hand were missing, and there was a bullet wound also in his left side. There were holes in his *pheran* [cape]. The army came shortly thereafter and took the body to the local police station where they filed an FIR claiming that Amin was a released militant who had been re-arrested to lead the army to an arms cache, and that he had done so. On returning to the camp, the FIR said, Amin tried to take one of those weapons and fire at the soldiers, upon which they killed him. I tried to fill an FIR, but the police said there already was an FIR. I tried to get a copy of it for the court, but the police refused to give me one.

Disappearances

Human rights groups in Kashmir have documented more than three hundred cases of "disappearances" since 1990. Lawyers believe the number to be far higher, however, as many relatives do not contact a lawyer out of fear of reprisal. Neither the Indian government nor any of the security agencies operating in the state has provided any information to clarify the whereabouts of the victim in any of these cases. It is likely that in virtually all of the cases of "disappearances" in Kashmir, the victim was executed and the body disposed of in secret.

Since 1996, the Association of the Parents of the Disappeared has worked to put pressure on state and central government authorities to account for some 300 cases of "disappearance." As of June 1999, the association had yet to obtain clarification on a single case, however. The head of the organization, Parveen Akhtar, told Human Rights Watch about her own efforts to obtain nformation about the whereabouts of her son, Javed Ahmad Ahangar, who was sixteen when he "disappeared" on August 18, 1991. According to Ahangar, the High Court has ordered the prosecution of three army officers responsible, but as of June 1999, no action had been taken.

The security forces routinely flout legal protections that would provide a safeguard against "disappearances." Detainees are frequently shifted from one detention facility to another, sometimes under the authority of different security agencies;

records of arrest are either not kept or are falsified; and the security forces ignore writs of habeas corpus and refuse to produce detainees even when ordered to do so by the Jammu and Kashmir High Court. According to the Jammu and Kashmir Bar Association, as of May 1999, hundreds of habeas corpus petitions remained pending before the court, some dating back several years.

Abdul-Ahad Dar

Abdul-Ahad Dar was taken from his residence in Halmatpora, Kupwara, by the STF on the night of July 4-5, 1995. The force was headed by the Kupwara Superintendent of Police (SP) Manhas, who has since been posted elsewhere in the state. Another man who was arrested with Dar was released after a few days. The police interrogated Dar as to the whereabouts of his brother, who they claimed was a militant.

Dar's wife went to the chief judicial magistrate of Kupwara and asked him to tell her why her husband was arrested and where he was being detained. The court orderd the STF to respond, and the STF replied that it had arrested him but had released him the next day. A lawyer for the family then filed a petition before the High Court, number 400\95. The court again ordered the state to respond, and this time the STF claimed that it had never arrested Dar. The lawyer then submitted the Kupwara court document to the High Court. It was not until 1997, however, that the court ordered an official inquiry directed by the chief judicial magistrate of Sopore. During the inquiry, the other detainee, who had been released after a few days, was produced before the court, and he testified that Abdul-Ahad Dar had in fact been arrested at the same time by SP Manhas.

In 1998, after the court session in Sopore, the witness who had testified to Dar's arrest was detained for a day by the STF, who apparently pressured him to change his story. According to the lawyer, SP Manhas then tried to get the witness to return to the Sopore court, but the magistrate refused to allow him to appear again as he had already testified and had beencross-examined. The SP then took the witness to the Kupwara court, where he obtained anaffidavit from him in which he retracted his story. This affidavit has now been produced before the Sopore court, leaving it with two conflicting statements.

According to the lawyer, Dar's wife has complained that since July 1998, whenever she has tried to go to court in Sopore, which is about forty kilometers from her home, she is stopped by the STF who tell her not to go to the court and promise to resolve the case for her. In early October 1998, an official told her he would pay her Rs. 50,000 [U.S.$1,250] if she agreed to say that the police did release her husband and that he was subsequently killed by militants. Her lawyer told Human Rights Watch that he feared that the wife, who has small children to care for, had lost hope and might ultimately accept the money.

Ashiq Husein Malik
In an interview with Human Rights Watch, Q., stated that on the evening of May 23, 1997, he witnessed the arrest of Ashiq Husein Malik at his home in Peerbagh Hyderpora, Srinagar. At 11:00 p.m., soldiers of the 20th Grenadiers Rashtriya Rifles came to the house with an unidentified informer. They ordered Malik to come with them and find Ghulam Qadir Bhat, also in the village. They went to Bhat's house, and then left with both Malik and Bhat.

The next day and from then on, Malik's family went to a number of police stations and army camps to look for them, but could not locate them. They tried to file an FIR, but the superintendent of the Badgam police station refused to register the case. Q. told Human Rights Watch:

Ghulam [Bhat] was released after five days and said he had been badly tortured and that Ashiq [Malik] had been with him during those five days. When Ghulam was released, he was brought in an army vehicle, and he told us that Ashiq had also been in that vehicle. That's the last we heard of him. I don't know why Ghulam was released and Ashiq was not.

According to the bar association, Malik had previously been arrested in 1995 and released. After he was again arrested and "disappeared" in 1997, his lawyer filed a petition with the High Court. The state counsel asked for a week's delay, which the judge granted. But that same day, after the family's lawyer had left the court, the state counsel submitted a response stating that Malik had been released in 1995, that is, after his first arrest. On the basis of that response, the judge dismissed the case.

Mushtaq Ahmad Dar, Mushtaq Ahmad Khan, Meraj Din Dar, Mohamed Sha'ban Khan, Mohamed Yahya Khan, Shabir Ahmad Dar, Bilal Ahmad Sheikh, and Nizar Ahmad Wani

Over a period of about a month between March and April 1997, at least eight men were arrested in the Batmaloo area on the outskirts of Srinagar by the Alpha Company, Boatmen Colony Unit, of the Indian army. As of June 1999, the whereabouts of all eight remained unknown. In several of the cases, the army has since denied arresting the men.

F., a villager from Tengapura, Batmaloo, Srinagar, told Human Rights Watch that at midnight on the night of April 13, 1997, a force of twenty grenadiers of the

Alpha Company, Boatmen Colony Unit, came to the house of Mushtaq Ahmad Khan, twenty-five, the son of Mohamed Sultan Khan. The force was headed by an officer named Sahb Singh, who wore two stars on his uniform, and a second officer of the Central Bureau of Intelligence (CBI). Mushtaq Khan was taken from his bed and put in a room by himself, where he was interrogated by the two officers. His family, including F., was locked in a room and beaten. That same night, another resident of Tengapura, Mushtaq Ahmad Dar, the son of Ghulam Mohamed Dar, was arrested by the same raiding party and interrogated. MushtaqDar had been in prison twice before and released. Both men were taken to an unknown location and have not been seen or heard from since.

The next day, April 14, the family of Mushtaq Ahmad Khan filed an FIR with the Shergali police station. They also went to the inspector general of police, the director general of police, the Central Bureau of Investigation, the army headquarters, and the Alpha Company based in Bimna, Srinagar. None of the security forces acknowledged taking the men.

On April 18, the same unit headed by the same officers arrested Meraj Din Dar, the son of Abderrazzaq Dar, who was also a resident of Tengapura. The family has not been able to locate him since. He was a released militant who had spent two and a half years in prison. After his release he was managing a shoe store out of his home.

Also on the night of April 18, Mohamed Sha'ban Khan, who was in his forties, and his son, Mohamed Yahya Khan, twenty-five, were arrested in Nasrullahpura, Bargam, seven kilometers from Tengapura. They were taken by the same military unit to an unknown location. The father-in-law of Mohamed Sha'ban Khan filed a suit in the High Court and lodged a complaint with the National Human Rights Commission in New Delhi. On January 1, 1998, the NHRC ordered the Ministry of Defense to respond no later than February 16, 1998. In a response to the High Court appeal, the government stated that it had never arrested the men. The High Court ordered an inquiry, the results of which were not available to Human Rights Watch as of June 1999.

In early April, about a week before the arrest of the Mushtaq Ahmad Khan and Mushtaq Ahmad Dar, two young men, Shabir Ahmad Dar, twenty-three, son of Ghulam Nabi Dar, resident of Gangabuk, Srinagar, and Bilal Ahmad Sheikh, twenty-one, son of Ali Mohamed Sheikh, were arrested on the bypass road that separates Tengapura from Srinagar proper. They were walking along the road when members of the same unit in a military truck picked them up. The families have been unable to locate them since. Shabir's father filed a case before the High Court.

Nizar Ahmad Wani, seventeen or eighteen, the son of Ghulam Mohamed Wani, a bicycle repairman of Diarwani, Batmaloo, was arrested by the same unit in March 1997. As of June 1999, his whereabouts remained unknown.

Bashir Ahmad Wani and Bashir Ahmad Bhat

Ghulam Nabi Wani, a resident of Mandak Pal village, Pampore, stated that on November 18, 1997, Station House Officer (SHO) M. S. Jindral summoned Wani's son, Bashir Ahmad Wani, in his early twenties, to appear at the local police station the next day. On November 19, a large group of people from the neighborhood accompanied him and his father to the police station. They were told that he would be released again after a little while. He was held in the police station for four days, during which his family was not allowed to see him. He wasthen transferred to the Lethpora interrogation center. Shortly thereafter, another young man from the neighborhood, Bashir Ahmad Bhat, also in his early twenties, was arrested on November 24.

When Bashir Ahmad Wani was not released as promised, his family petitioned the High Court, and the court ordered the SHO to release the men. But on July 14, 1998, the High Court dismissed the case after state counsel informed the court that both men had been found innocent and released on November 23. Because the family's lawyer was unable to come to the court that day, the family could not counter the state counsel's assertions. But the men were not released; in fact, Bashir Ahmad Bhat was not even arrested until November 24. The lawyer for the Wani family then filed a new appeal, and according to the bar association, when the High Court ordered the state to respond, the state claimed that the detainees were released in the custody of two notables from the village. As evidence, it produced a statement supposedly signed by these two notables, stating that the two men were indeed released into their custody. The statement also carried the signature of one of the missing men. The lawyer for the family told Human Rights Watch that he suspected that the signatures were forged, as the two notables have disavowed any knowledge of the matter. Moreover, the missing person could not have signed his name as he cannot write; he normally would have marked the document with his thumbprint instead.

Both families have also filed a case with the State Human Rights Commission, as the case involves the police, not the army, and therefore falls within the jurisdiction of the SHRC.

Mohammad Iqbal

Human Rights Watch also received information about the "disappearance" of Mohammad Iqbal, the son of Abdul Rehman Malik, residents of Bharat Doda. Mohammad Iqbal Malik was employed as a deputy forestry officer. According to his brother, Mohammad Yaseen Malik, on the night of June 27-28, 1996, Mohammad Iqbal Malik was arrested from the Darul Iqbal rest house, extension Raj Bagh Srinagar, by Major Balbir of the 7th Rashtriya Rifles based at Camp Wailoo, Kukarnag, in Anantnag district. Major Balbir was accompanied by two countermilitants, Abdul Rashid Rather, also known as Amir Raja, and Fiaz Ahmed Ganai, of the Ikhwan-ul Muslimoon militia. When Mohammad Yaseen inquired about his brother's whereabouts, he was sometimes told that Mohammad Iqbal was in the Qazi Gund headquarters of the 7th Rashtriya Rifles. At other times he was told that

Mohammad Iqbal was being held at Camp Wailoo or at Larkipura Camp. He stated:

Since then I have been searching for my brother everywhere ... but all in vain. Now more than two and a half years have passed, but I do not know the whereabouts of my brother.

Torture

Torture has been used routinely by all the security forces operating in Kashmir. Although the problem is widely known to the authorities in Srinagar and New Delhi, neither has ever made any serious effort to curb it. When questioned, officials frequently respond that they have no other alternative to deal with terrorists who do not respect the law. Torture is used to extract information, to punish detainees and to try to force detainees to become informers or to join countermilitant organizations. It is also used to extort money from the victim's family. The choice of certain forms of torture appears to be indiscriminate; while some detainees are subjected to a range of brutal torture techniques for no obvious reason, others may be subjected solely to beatings.

The most common forms of torture include severe beatings and electric shock. Detainees have also had their legs stretched apart, have been suspended from the wrists or upside down for extended periods, which can lead toparalysis, and have had an iron rod coated with chili paste inserted into the rectum. According to local doctors, this last can cause serious injury and infection when, as a result of pushing, the rod ruptures the bladder.

One of the most insidious forms of torture is the use of a heavy log or roller to apply excruciating pressure to the detainee's legs. The roller is rotated over the victim's legs, sometimes weighed down by a number of policemen who sit or stand on it. The practice has been widely used by police in India, notably in Punjab. Extensive use of the roller frequently leads to kidney damage. Severe beatings may also induce kidney failure, as can electric shock because the contractions caused by the shocks as well as the trauma, which leads the muscles to release toxins that the kidneys cannot handle in large quantities. The risk of permanent injury is exacerbated by the fact that the victims are often denied water during interrogation and frequently become dehydrated. Since the conflict began in 1990, doctors in Kashmir have documented hundreds of cases of torture-induced renal failure in Kashmir.

Human Rights Watch interviewed four doctors in Kashmir who have treated torture victims. Estimates varied, but of the four, estimates ranged from three to eight cases a week. Sources at the Soura Medical Institute in Srinagar told us that they had registered more than 180 patients with torture-induced renal problems since 1994, some one hundred of which were admitted since 1996. These figures only include those cases serious enough to require treatment in the hospital. Of the 180 cases, six died of renal failure. Some of the survivors have suffered permanent damage. According to the doctors, those most at risk include persons with lowered immunity who may suffer kidney damage after even a mild beating. Those who have received treatment for torture-induced renal problems have been mostly young males but have included some older men.

According to one doctor familiar with the problem:

People who come to see me with torture-inflicted injuries are often so afraid that they virtually beg me not to reveal the facts of their case to my colleagues... You wonder how many cases don't come to the hospital at all. We usually only get the most severe cases. The most frequent torture cases I see are soft-tissue injuries: the use of the roller, gun butts, sticks, and kicks with pointed boots. When a person gets hit this way, a liquid is released that is toxic to the kidneys. To rinse it out people need to drink a lot, and the problem is that in the interrogation centers the detainees are not given sufficient water.

He estimated that renal failure occurred in about 5 percent of the cases.

J., October 1998

When Human Rights Watch was in Srinagar on October 18, 1998, the army conducted a cordon-and-search operation (known as a crackdown) in the Sariballa neighborhood of the city. This operation occurred a day after a grenade was thrown at a nearby bunker, injuring a BSF officer. Human Rights Watch interviewed J., twenty-five, one of the men from the neighborhood who had been detained during the crackdown, interrogated and released. J. had been sitting in a park with two friends waiting to see a movie and a nearby theater when army officers pulled up and order them into the vehicle. J. stated:

They didn't ask us any questions. They blindfolded us with a piece of cloth and took us to the Badimai Bagh camp in the Batwara area of Srinagar. They didn't ask us for our identity cards. They just said to us: "Give us the weapons. Show us where the weapons are." When we replied that wedidn't have any weapons, they started beating us, and this lasted for about an hour and a half. We were beaten non-stop. They used belts, boots, and thick sticks. They were five army soldiers, and they just kept asking us for the weapons. There was also an officer there, the commanding officer, who was in civilian clothes; he was asking the questions and also was beating us. Our hands were cuffed with metal cuffs and our feet as well. We were lying on the ground. We were wearing our clothes. They beat me on the soles of my feet and on top of my feet as well with sticks. They also pulled some skin off my forehead and near my elbow with pliers.

Human Rights Watch saw the scars on J.'s forehead, arm, back and soles of his feet. J. stated that because the beatings were so bad, he and his friends finally told the security forces that they had weapons. The security forces then accompanied them back here to their homes. J. continued:

When we got here, they told us to show them where we had hidden the weapons, so we said that we didn't have any. We were here two and a half hours. One of my two friends was taken out of the vehicle and led into his home. They told his mother that if her son refused to show them where the weapons were they would kill him. I was taken into the house of other people, whom they asked to identify me as a militant. I was beaten in that house for about an hour. And they were still asking the same question.

Then they took all three back to the same camp. After about an hour, the same officer came and began to lecture them, saying: "Don't support the militancy! Why did you tell me earlier that you have weapons?" They then released them at about 8:30 p.m. They were treated at the Bone and Joint Hospital and released. Documents Human Rights Watch obtained from the hospital confirmed that there had been trauma particularly to J.'s feet.

When Human Rights Watch interviewed J. two days after his arrest, he could stand only with great difficulty. He bore the marks of a severe beating on his back and feet and had lesions on his forehead, and said that he was still in great pain.

X

X., twenty-five, a resident of Anchar, a neighborhood on the outskirts of Srinagar, was first arrested in November 1995. He was detained and tortured at various jails and interrogation centers for three years. He was picked up from the street in the Hapt Chinar neighborhood of Srinagar, where he was visiting relatives. At about 3:00 p.m., the 12th Battalion of the BSF from Karanagar camp carried out a raid in that area. As they arrested him, one soldier struck him on the nose with his rifle butt, fracturing it. They took him to the interrogation center at Karanagar camp. There he was interrogated for two months continuously. After four months he was moved to the Papa II interrogation center in Srinagar, from where he was transferred to Kortbulwal jail and then to Udhampur jail, where he was held for one year. On April 17, 1997, he was moved to Jammu central jail, where he stayed until November 1997. Then he was transferred back to Kortbulwal until January 1998. From there he was taken to the Harinawas interrogation center in Srinagar for four days, and then to Rangrat jail in Srinagar. On April 20, 1998, he was taken to the police station in Soura, where he stayed for three days before he was granted bail. X. recalled:

The first two months were very bad. They said they wanted me to take them to the weapons. I told them I had never touched a weapon and that I had no connection to the militants. They wanted me to tell them the locations of the militants. In Karanagar they hung me upside down. They burned parts of my leg and foot with a torch. They stuck a metal pin in my penis and sent a current from a battery through it. They also used the roller on my legs. I was interrogated also in Papa II and Papa I, and then in Udhampur. Each time they questioned me they used electricity. It happened countless times... Udhampur was particularly bad. The guards there were very brutal. They were always beating me even when they knew I was ill. I couldn't even walk at the time. When I was in Udhampur I also temporarily lost my sight in my right eye, while my other eye was all blurry. I couldn't see at all. This lasted about six months. I don't know what brought it on.

X. showed Human Rights Watch the fading scars on his legs, feet and neck. He could hardly walk and then only with the aid of a cane. At the time of the interview, X. still had no sensation in his left arm.

While X. was in jail in Jammu, he was examined by a doctor who referred him for admittance to a hospital. At the government medical college hospital in Jammu, doctors examined X.'s nose and left arm, which has become paralyzed in Udhampur jail. He was then returned to Jammu jail. X. told Human Rights Watch that after his release he received treatment and recovered his sight but continued to have episodes of dizziness.

Undermining the Judiciary

Kashmir's judiciary has been virtually unable to provide any recourse for victims of human rights violations or relief for their families because security personnel routinely flout laws and procedures that would afford detainees and witnesses some protection. Authorities admit that if cases were to come before the courts under normal procedures, it would be extremely difficult to convict suspected militants. A lawyer for the Jammu and Kashmir Bar Association told Human Rights Watch that acquittal rates in such cases neared 100 percent, principally because the government is unable to find witnesses willing to testify against the detainees; most would not do so out of fear of retaliation from militant groups, or out of solidarity.

In response, the government avoids courts to the extent possible, either by detaining suspects indefinitely by administrative means or by killing them. The Public Safety Act allows for a non-renewable two-year detention without trial. Once the detention order expires, new charges are brought against the detainee, often based on an alleged crime committed in the early 1990s when the Terrorist and Disruptive Activities Act (TADA) was in effect. TADA provides for one year of detention without trial. When detainees appeal to the High Court, the court often orders the government to show cause or release the detainee, but to little effect. According to the bar association, the government has issued instructions now to the police not to comply with High Court rulings without informing the security forces first. If a detainee is set to be released, new charges are brought, and he is "re-arrested" on the new charges that permit periods of detention up to two years. As a result, detainees may be held indefinitely; the bar association has documented cases of detainees being held for six or more years despite multiple release or bail orders from the courts.

Driven by a need for greater deniability about their actions, in many cases the security forces avoid the court system entirely by summarily executing detainees and then portraying the event as a death during an armed encounter. In other cases the security forces simply deny ever having arrested the person. The practice of summarily executing or "disappearing" suspected militants has not changed since the early 1990s. Lawyers contend that hundreds of habeas corpus rulings ordering the security forces to produce detainees in court have been ignored. It is symptomaticof the magnitude of Kashmir's human rights crisis that such a fundamental protection under the law is treated by government officials with contempt.

Detention Practices that Facilitate Abuse

Most detainees in Kashmir are never formally arrested yet are detained for months or longer without charge. There are forty official detention centers in Kashmir; some detainees are also held outside the state in Delhi or Uttar Pradesh. In addition to the official centers, the government also operates some secret facilities.

In October 1997, the state government transferred the power of releasing detainees from prison authorities to the police. According to a human rights lawyer in the state, the result has been that prison authorities are no longer required to obey High Court orders to release a detainee even if the court determines that there are insufficient grounds for arrest. The police have final authority in such cases.

Detainees who are ultimately charged are generally charged under the Jammu and Kashmir Public Safety Act (PSA) or under the Terrorist and Disruptive Activities Act (TADA). Under the PSA, a detainee may be held in administrative detention for a maximum of two years without a court order. At the detainee's request, an advisory board consisting of three judges may be assembled to review the detainee's case. The detainee may make this request only once.

TADA has been widely used in Kashmir against persons suspected of having ties with militant groups. The act (as amended in 1987) authorizes administrative detention without formal charge or trial for up to one year. It virtually criminalizes free speech. Under the TADA, anyone who "knowingly facilitates the commission of any disruptive activity or any act preparatory to a disruptive activity shall be punishable with imprisonment for a term which shall not be less than three years but which may extend to a term of life and shall also be liable to fine." A disruptive activity includes "any action taken, whether by act or by speech or through any other media or in any other manner whatsoever, (i) which questions, disrupts or is intended to disrupt, whether directly or indirectly, the sovereignty and territorial integrity of India; or (ii) which is intended to bring about or supports any claim, whether directly or indirectly, for the cession of any part of India or the secession of any part of India from the Union." The provisions of TADA also substantially increase the risk of torture.

Although TADA lapsed in 1995, the security forces in Kashmir continue to charge detainees under TADA, claiming that the crime committed occurred before

TADA was repealed. According to a human rights lawyer in Kashmir, during the period when TADA was in force, many of the cases registered at police stations were vaguely worded and did not always link an alleged crime to a specific individual. A militant group would be accused of a particular violent act, but the individual members of this group were not necessarily named in the First Information Report (FIR). These cases have remained under investigation, even after the repeal of TADA, and suspects arrested since the repeal of TADA are frequently accused of having participated in the crime at the time the FIR wasregistered. In such cases, according to security officials, TADA continues to apply, and such suspects may be arrested under TADA. The courts in Kashmir have not challenged the retroactive use of TADA.

Human rights lawyers complain that there is little recourse available to them to intervene in cases of detention and "disappearance." If the whereabouts of the detainee are known but no charges have been filed, the lawyer may go to court and demand that the charge sheet-the formal registration of charges-be provided. In many cases, however, the whereabouts of the detainee are not known. In that case, a lawyer takes a habeas corpus petition to the High Court under Section 491 of the Criminal Procedures Code. If the government does not respond to the court's subsequent request to account for the person, or if the government claims it is not detaining the person, a district judge can order an *enquete* (inquiry). If the person is arrested under the Public Safety Act (PSA), there is a far better chance that the detainee will be produced in court than if he or she is detained under no specific charge. Screening committees which function at the district and state level review court orders and can decide to ignore orders for release or bail. If a detainee agrees during interrogation to join the countermilitants he may be released without a court order.

Detention of Nur Mohamed Kalwal

The case of Nur Mohamed Kalwal, a resident of Mir Muhalla, Nowhata, is illustrative. Kalwal, a leading member of the JKLF, was arrested by the CRPF on September 8, 1991. On February 29, 1992, he was placed under PSA detention for one year, which he spent in Udhampur jail. When his term expired on February 28, 1993, he was moved to the Joint Interrogation Center jail in Korbawal, Jammu but was not released. In 1993, his lawyer filed a petition for his release with the High Court; the case was registered as 387/93. The state failed to explain why Kalwal was not released In 1995 the High Court issued a directive that the state should either release Kalwal or produce him before the court. Although Kalwal was transferred to the subjail of Rangrate, apparently to bring him before the court, he was not produced in court. The High Court then initiated contempt proceedings against the state.

In 1996 the district magistrate issued a PSA order against Kalwal for one year. In 1997, his lawyer filed a petition with the High Court challenging this new order, and the High Court accepted the argument, set aside the PSA detention order, and ordered the detainee released. The state did not release him, however, but filed a charge against him at the TADA court under a 1991 FIR, namely that a revolver was lifted from him at the time of his arrest in 1991. This charge had never been mentioned before.

The lawyer approached the TADA court, which granted bail. The prosecution then showed to the judge a letter from Counter-Intelligence Kashmir (CIK) to the prosecutor saying that he should make sure that the detainee would not be physically released, and that if he were to be released, the CIK should be notified immediately. The prosecutor also showed a letter from the CIK to the central jail of Srinagar saying that if they received an order from the court for his release, they should inform the CIK immediately so that it could continue to detain him. Although Kalwal's lawyer was permitted to read the letters, the judge refused to make them public, claiming that they were private letters between two agencies outside the court.

As of the Human Rights Watch interview, Kalwal remained in jail, awaiting trial. His lawyer commented, "Each time he is brought to court, a CIK vehicle accompanies the vehicle in which he is transported, just to make sure they will nab him in case he gets set free."

Detention of Abdel Majid Gadyara, Mehraizin Gadyara and Farouq [last name unknown]

Abdel Majid Gadyara, a resident of Kalal Doori, Nidkadal, Srinagar, had been arrested by the security forces a number of times and released. On September 21, 1998, he was again detained, this time by the STF. After a lawyer for the family submitted a bail application, the chief judicial magistrate requested a charge sheet from the arresting STF officer. When the STF officer refused to provide the court with the charges, the court instituted proceedings against the officer for contempt of court and issued a warrant for his arrest on September 29. The STF officer responded to the warrant by stating that he was not liable for the charges because the detainee had been transferred to Safakadam police station and was no longer his responsibility. The chief judicial magistrate then moved the petition to the Court of Judicial Magistrate, City Munsif, Srinagar (a regular procedure), ordering Abdel Majid Gadyara released on bail, and he was so released on October 3.

In what was apparently a retaliatory move, on October 12 the STF arrested Abdel Majid's cousin Farouq, as well as Abdel Majid's younger brother Mehraizin. Mehraizin Gadyara had previously been detained on a number of occasions and held without charge. During his previous period of detention his legs had been broken during interrogation, and after he appealed to the State Human Rights Commission, he was released on bail. After the two were detained, the family's lawyer immediately filed a habeas corpus petition, and the STF then submitted the charges against the two men. They were charged with murder and possession of weapons under the Ranbir Penal Code, the Indian Arms Act, and the Enemy Agent Act. These offenses carry a possible death penalty.

Detention of Abdelaziz Dar

Abdelaziz Dar, forty, a resident of Saida Kadal, Raniwari, Srinagar, has been in custody since 1993, despite the fact that he completed his one year of administrative detention under the PSA in 1994. He is a leading member of the Jamaat-i Islami in Srinagar. His father was also with Jamaat-i Islami. Abdelaziz Dar was first arrested after the 1987 elections and was detained for a year without trial. After his release he became a district commander of the Hizb-ul Mujahidin and was again arrested on September 16, 1991, and detained for one year under PSA. He told Human Rights Watch that after his 1992 release, he continued to work with the Jamaat-i Islami but no longer with Hizb-ul Mujahidin. He was again arrested on February 1, 1993 and detained for one year under the PSA. His administrative detention was completed in June 1994, but he was not released. He has not been told the reason. Although the High Court ordered him released on bail, as did two TADA courts, one on November 7, 1996, and one on February 24, 1997, he has been kept in jail under his original file, 1/92. Justice A. M. Mir of the High Court noted in a statement ordering Dar's release that "any detention after a bail order having been passed and served will be wrongful in the eye of law."

The various security forces cooperate with each other to instill fear and ensure compliance from the local population. G. told Human Rights Watch that in January 1997, following a number of explosions on the road to the airport, the local BSF commander questioned his son, who had a shop in the market, about who was behind the blasts. After this had happened a few times, the BSF took the son into custody.

The next day I went to see senior BSF officers. They gave me a polite but comprehensive warning that I should cooperate with the security forces or face the consequences, in light of the fact, they said, that my son had confessed to having links with foreign militants. Now there were Afghani militants coming to the store, so I told them that there was nothing I could do about that: Afghans come to the store, as does the military. I couldn't stop them. After a little while, the senior officerstook me to the commanding officer at Totuground, an interrogation center in Srinagar. The commanding officer repeated the charge that my son had connections with the militants ... So then I told him that if my son would confirm the same in my presence, I would not object to whatever lawful punishment they would choose to mete out to him. He told me: "We want to be lenient, provided that you cooperate with us in normalizing the military situation and provide information." I then repeated that if my son had confessed, he should be punished, and asked that I be allowed to ask my son this question. He agreed to that, so I asked my son, "What did you tell him?" And my son said that Afghani militants sometimes come to the store, and he could not help this.

The BSF officers then produced an informer who claimed that the son had contacts with the militants. G. questioned the informer, who admitted he did not have information about the son. The son was released that evening. However, half an hour later, the house was surrounded by the local Rashtriya Rifles unit, accompanied by countermilitant forces, who told G. to hand over his son and threatened to throw explosives into the house if he did not. G. left the house to tell a local journalist, who called the army public relations office to complain. G. stated:

As I reached my home, the Rashtriya Rifles party and renegades [countermilitants] were withdrawing, but not before telling me that they would be back by 10:00 p.m., and if my son wasn't there, there would be real damage. At this point, all the members of my extended family, seventeen persons, fled the house, as did some of the neighbors from their homes, fearing blasts. At 10:00 p.m., the party returned; I was alone in the house. My son was not there. They were a bit more polite now and said they would return at 8:00 the next morning. And they did show up the next morning, this time without the renegades. My son was still not there. Then they drew a survey map of my house and shop and left. Immediately afterwards, the BSF officer who had arrested my son came to the house. He was friendly and courteous. He told me that my son and I were in big trouble, as the army [the Rashtriya Rifles] had taken over the case: "They are ruthless. So you'd better follow my directions, as the army will listen to me. You should make sure to keep your neighborhood free of militancy. And keep your son away until you get further instructions." I acted accordingly. I spent four miserable days before deciding to send my son to Delhi for safety reasons. He stayed there for six months. He came back in July 1997 and must report once a month to the BSF to account for his activities. In the meantime, as my son wasn't there, I had to sell the shop ... I did have to concede a little on one thing. I said I couldn't account for the neighborhood, but that they had nothing to worry about from my family's compound.

Detentions for Extortion

S., a shopkeeper in Srinagar, told the story of his neighbor, Rashad Ahmad Sheikh, eighteen, son of Mohamed Amin Sheikh, a resident of Babademb, Srinagar. Rashad was arrested by the local police of the Soura station in August 1998. He was not accused of any crime; the police apparently arrested him in extort money from his father, who was told to pay Rs. 30,000 [U.S. $750] in order to get his son released. That same night, the police also arrested another boy, Muzaffer Ahmad Najar, son of Mohamed Sultan Najar. But the father paid the SHO at Soura police station, and his son was released. Rashad's father, who earns only Rs 3,000 [U.S. $75] a month, could not afford to pay, so after about a month he went to the local court, but his son was not released. Under pressure from the police, Rashad reportedly confessed to having a grenade in his possession and faces prolonged detention under those charges.

In a similar incident, Aijaz Ahmad Karwar, about twenty-three, son of Ghulam Ahmad Karwar, who was also a resident of Babademb, Srinagar, was arrested on or about October 5, 1998, by police from the Zaina Kadal police station who were looking for his brother, Javed, about twenty-eight, who was believed to be with a militant group in Pakistan. Aijaz Karwar himself was not accused of any crime, nor was he asked to produce his brother. But the police have told his father, who visits him daily, to pay them Rs. 100,000 [U.S.$2,500] for his son's release. His father is a government employee with a salary of Rs. 6,000 to 7,000 [U.S.$150-175] per month and cannot afford this amount. Aijaz Karwar also works for the government as a junior engineer, earning roughly the same amount. S. described the father's reaction:

After seeing his son, he was crying and saying things like: "First I lost my oldest son, now my second one is in jail." All the neighbors went to see the state home minister, Mushtaq Lone, to provide guarantees that Aijaz was not a militant, but the minister referred the case to the SP [Superintendent of Police] of Srinagar. They then went to the SP, but he said he could not release Aijaz at this time. He told them to wait until November 1 after the government has left for Jammu. Then he would see what he could do.

Abuses Involving Counter militant Militias

Since at least early 1995, Indian security forces have been making systematic use of state-sponsored countermilitary forces, frequently called "renegades" by Kashmiris, composed of captured or surrendered former militants, in effect subcontracting some of their abusive tactics to groups with no official accountability. Many of these groups have been responsible for grave human rights abuses, including summary executions, "disappearances," torture, and illegal detention. Although the Indian government routinely denies any responsibility for the actions of these groups, they are organized and armed by the Indian army and other security forces and operate under their command and protection. The government uses the groups principally to assassinate and intimidate members of militant organizations and political groups, especially the banned pro-Pakistan party Jamaat-i Islami.

Government officials have described the recruitment of former militants as a rehabilitation program. However, members of these groups move about openly carrying automatic weapons, in full view of security personnel, even though under the government's rehabilitation program, all surrendered militants are required to hand over their weapons. Indian army forces routinely carry out patrols and other operations accompanied by members of such groups.

The state-sponsored groups operate with impunity. Even if arrested by the local police, countermilitants are invariably released after the intervention of the army or BSF. The countermilitants operate in close proximity to army and BSF camps, and some have been housed in the camps.

On October 14, 1998, the army commander, Gen. Krishna Pal, attended a meeting at which he lauded one of the principal countermilitant groups, Ikhwan-ul Muslimoon (Muslim Brotherhood), and then laid a wreath at the grave of Wafa Dar Khan, the Ikhwan's supreme commander who was killed by a landmine earlier in the year. In a statement released by the government's Press Information Bureau, the army

acknowledge[d] the supreme sacrifices made and the services rendered by members of the JK Ikhwan in helping restore peace and normalcy in the Kashmir

Valley... The Corps Commander reiterated that the army will continue to extend full support to the JK Ikhwan ... Gen. Krishan Pal saidthat the Ikhwan are the eyes and the ears of the security forces and that they have a very important role to play in defeating the proxy war being waged on Kashmir soil.

Human Rights Watch interviewd Papa Kishtwari, the local leader of Ikhwan-ul Muslimoon in Pampore, whose real name is Ghulam Hassan Lone. His house lies on the main road from Srinagar to the military airport and is guarded by CRPF men as well as Ikhwan members toting automatic weapons. Before the insurgency broke out in Kashmir, he was a junior officer in the CRPF. He then became a commander in the Al-Jihad militant group before being imprisoned. He told Human Rights Watch that he was detained for twenty-one months in 1993-95, during which time he was tortured with electric shocks to his penis. His interrogators also forced gasoline into his rectum. After his release he joined Ikhwan. He told Human Rights Watch:

We [the countermilitants] were brought out to crush the militants. We paved the way for the 1996 elections... Now I am a politician. Sometimes we work with the army as informers in operations, an activity for which we get some money. I have 366 men working for me in Kashmir. We go along with army personnel when they have received information that a certain militant is hiding in such and such a place. We will assist in the arrest, and if there is an encounter, we will fight. But I never go myself, and I don't touch a weapon...My boys ... are special police officers and will remain so. They get Rs. 1,500 [$37.50] per month from the government.

Kishtwari provided Human Rights Watch with a picture of himself and Indian army officers in front of weapons supposedly captured from militants. Upon request, he signed the back and stamped it with the symbol of his political party, Tahreek Wattan.

Sources who spoke to HRW on the basis of confidentiality stated that they believed Kishtwari's group to be responsible for the March 1996 extrajudicial execution of Ghulam Rasool, a young journalist who had attempted to expose other killings he believed had been committed by Papa Kishtwari in Pampore. Rasool had been the head of the local *waqf* committee, which oversees local schools and mosques. In an October 1998 interview with Human Rights Watch, Kishtwari denied allegations that he and his group have been responsible for extrajudicial killings:

That's all propaganda. What I have done is create an atmosphere of fear in which people believe that I will in fact kill the militants. But my duty is to arrest militants, rehabilitate them, and provide them with jobs once they are released. Because of this policy of mine of instilling fear, there no longer is any militancy in Pampore. About these allegations, if there is any evidence against me, then show me any FIR and I will accept guilt. I told the people this in both elections, which I lost.

The following cases are illustrative of the countermilitants' practice of targeting Jamaat-i Islami members and others who have stood up to them and, in these cases, driving them from their homes. In all three cases, the operations were carried out jointly by Ikhwan and army forces.

Threats against T

T, thirty-nine, is a teacher and former resident of Aloosa, Banipura, a town about seventy-five kilometers from Srinagar with about 10-15,000 residents. He told Human Rights Watch that on May 23, 1995, a girl from the village named Farida was abducted by a countermilitant named Mohamed Sarwar Bhat who wanted to marry her against the will of the girl and her family. The girl was already engaged. Bhat had taken her to another village, Sopura, Barimula. T. managed to negotiate the girl's release on May 25. T. then returned to his place of work, which was in another village, in Kupwara district. After a month, on June 24, T. returned to his home village, Aloosa. Later that same day, a party of Ikhwan and the 15th Rashtriya Rifles came to his house, but T. was not there at the time. After he learned that they had been looking for him, he left the village the next day and has not returned since, although his wife, daughters, mother, and sister are all still living there. When his father died on October 28,

1997, T. was told that the security forces had put out word that he could not go back for the funeral. After the incident, T. found a teaching job elsewhere. He has only seen his family once after his wife and children made the three-and-a-half hour trip to Srinagar. He has approached the army to try to get permission to go back, but they would not give it. He believes that Ikhwan told the army that he was working with the militants.

T. told Human Rights Watch that two other men have been forced out of the village by the renegades: Abderrahman Bhat, forty-five, and Abdelghani Wani, a man in his seventies. T. told HRW:

If the army weren't there, I could go back. The renegades by themselves are not a problem. They are a problem only when the army backs them.

Threats against the Family of X

X., a resident of Midoora, Tral, Pulwana, told Human Rights Watch that one evening in early February 1996, at about 6:30 p.m., he was with his father in the mosque, which is about one hundred meters from his house, when some ten to fifteen Ikhwan members and two vehicles full of army soldiers came to the house. The soldiers belonged to the 3rd Gurkha Regiment based in a camp some two kilometers from the village.

When they first arrived in the village, they started firing into the air and shouting at the people who were outside. They broke down the doors of our house and windows and removed everything from inside, including utensils, bedding, clothing and jewelry. After forty-five minutes, they left.

The next day, the family filed an FIR. About two weeks later, an army patrol returned to the house at about 3:00 p.m. and removed anything that was left including the doors and door frames. The family was living elsewhere at the time. X. believed that the reason for the destruction was that the elder man in the house supports the Jamaat-i Islami. He stated that four other houses belonging to Jamaat-i Islami supporters in the village were similarly ransacked.

Threats against Mehraj-u-Din Bhat

Mehraj-u-Din Bhat, twenty-two, a photographer who lives in Ajas, Sonawari, Baramula, told Human Rights Watch that he was arrested by the army (the 10th Bihar Regiment) on April 6, 1992 because of his affiliations with the Jamaat-i Islami. He was released after sixteen months. After that, the army would detain him monthly for two or three days.

They would come to my studio and take me with them. Always they were asking me to work for them, and I refused every time. This continued until September 1998. In this period, the army units changed, but not the pattern of my detentions: whoever was there picked me up, once a month.

On June 4, 1998, about fifteen army personnel and ten Ikhwan militia members in four vehicles came to Bhat's studio at about 9:30 a.m. At the time, he was taking photographs of children at the school next door, so he stayed inside the school and watched. The troops went into the shop and took a video camera worth Rs. 45,000 [U.S.$1,000], three still cameras worth Rs. 30,000 [$660], albums, and picture frames. The total value of stock and equipment taken came to Rs. 150,000 [$3,300]. The troops then set fire to the studio, and the entire shop burned to the ground. Bhat managed to repair the damage, but he learned that on September 14, 1998, some troops from Ikhwan and the army came back to the studio looking for him. He was not there at the time. They locked the shop. The next evening, September 15, at about 8:30 p.m., they came to Bhat's house. Again, he was not there. He stated that the troops left a note which said: "Leave the house immediately or you will be killed." After that, the family left the village. Bhat claimed that three other residents of the village were driven from their homes: a teacher named Mohamed Sakhi, Mumtaz Ahmad Rathor, a government employee, and another man named Abdelkhaliq Rathor. All were reportedly sympathetic to Jamaat-i Islami.

Threats against Human Rights Defenders

The killing of four of Kashmir's most prominent human rights activists in 1992, 1993 and 1996 deterred other human rights activists from carrying out documentation and advocacy work. Those who have continued to try to do so have been harassed and threatened. Some have been detained and tortured.

H. N. Wanchoo, a retired trade unionist and a communist, had documented cases of torture, extrajudicial executions, and disappearances and together with a local lawyer had brought these cases to the attention of the High Court and international human rights organizations. He was assassinated by unidentified gunmen on December 5, 1992. Because Wanchoo was a Hindu, the government found his work particularly embarrassing; it could not dismiss him as a militant. Although Indian officials claimed that the persons responsible were members of "a fundamentalist organization," human rights activists who investigated the case have alleged that two members of the militant organization Jamiat-ul Mujahidin were released from jail on condition that they kill Wanchoo. At least one of the militants was subsequently killed by Indian security forces. Dr. Farooq Ashai, a medical doctor who documented cases of torture and other abuses, was shot and killed by the CRPF on February 18, 1993. At the time, he was traveling in a car clearly marked with a red cross. Dr. Abdul Ahad Guru, a renowned Kashmiri cardiothoracic surgeon, was abducted and later shot dead on March

31, 1993. Dr. Guru was a member of the governing council of the JKLF and an outspoken critic of human rights abuses by Indian security forces in Kashmir. He met frequently with the international press and international human rights groups. A government source subsequently alleged to Human Rights Watch that Zulkar Nan, a militant member of the Hizb-ul Mujahidin, had been released specifically to carry out the murder. Shortly afterwards, Indian security forces shot and killed Zulkar Nan. The murder of Jalil Andrabi, a lawyer and leading member of the JKLF, is discussed below.

Torture of R.

R., a human rights activist, has been arrested three times since November 1995 and detained for periods of a few days during which he was badly tortured. He has never been charged or tried. On all three occasions he wasaccused of helping the militancy in some way.

During his interrogations he was frequently questioned about his human rights work.

R. was first arrested on November 2, 1995. He was held for five days by the BSF before a screening committee consented to his release. The second time was on May 19, 1996, just days before the first round of national parliamentary elections. He was arrested at 9:00 p.m. by Major Raju of the 7th Jat Regiment of the army, an officer well known in the neighborhood, and questioned about acquaintances who were known to be activists. R. was taken to a temporary army camp at Bagat-i-Kanapori in Srinagar and questioned about his links to the militant groups. He was also questioned about his human rights activities, his contact with Hurriyat leaders, and about the election boycott supported by the Hurriyat. The next day, the major, accompanied by his commanding officer, repeated the questions and then threatened R. with force if he did not cooperate. They left and then returned after an hour, when they repeated the same questions. Then they ordered their men to use force. R. described what happened next:

I was taken by the major and four subordinates to a small room, four by six feet, possibly a bathroom, with marble tiles on the floor and the walls. They stripped me down except for my underwear, and tied my hands and legs. They took a thick wooden roller and placed it under my knees as I was sitting. Then they told me to put my arms underneath the roller and up, and they tied my hands above my legs. I was like a football. Then they started kicking me and beating me with *lathis* [truncheons]. Then they began repeating those same questions. They got very frustrated, because I wasn't telling them anything I hadn't already told them. They also asked me: "How many Afghanis are in your home? Which militant leaders do you know?" Then they put a cloth in my mouth and spread another cloth over my face. I was lying on the floor facing the ceiling. They poured water into a bucket and then they poured the bucket out over my face. The water went into my nostrils, completely choking me. I was desperate to get out of that situation. I lost consciousness. When I came to, they were saying: "Now tell the truth! Cooperate!" I told them I would, so they gave me a few minutes to recover, but then the thing repeated itself. Again I lost consciousness; perhaps this was a longer spell, I'm not sure, but when I came to, I was exhausted. The major was patting my cheeks and saying my name. At first I couldn't recognize him. Then the major signalled for someone to come, and he brought a small magnet-type telephone box: when you turn the crank, a current shoots through the wires. They attached one wire to my left earlobe and the other to different places: one of my toes, my other ear, and my penis. They ran the current, and I lost consciousness again. When I came to, I noticed that my whole body was wet: I had urinated and defecated. I was taken to a bathroom outside the house, was given a bucket of water and told to clean myself up. I couldn't stand or stretch my arms. They helped me do some exercises for about two hours, and then I was able to stand up again and sit.

That night R.'s interrogators permitted a friend of his to come see him. After that, the major again told R. to come work for the army and stop his other activities. The next morning R. was taken to some other officials with one of the intelligence agencies. He was taken to the headquarters of the Jat Regiment. The commanding officer, Colonel Sharma, lectured him for an hour about the need to work for the army. When he was released on May 21 he was told to report to the camp every third day. He did so for about six weeks, and each time he was questioned again about his activities. After that, he received permission from Colonel Sharma not to report to the camp.

R. was detained for a third time in February 1998. At midnight on the night of February 2, fifteen to twenty members of the Special Operations Group (SOG), a police unit, came to his house, accompanied by some officers, escorted by the CRPF, and some intelligence people in military clothes. They searched the house and took all of his copies of human rights reports and some religious books. They took R. to SOG headquarters in Srinagar, where he was kept for the night. R. stated:

Then the torture started. They didn't tie me, but they rolled a big wooden roller over my leg muscles as I was lying down, and they passed electricity through me- one wire attached to a toe, the other to my penis-while they were questioning me. They asked me about my links with Asia Watch and Amnesty International. I told them everything I had done and who I had been in touch with, because this is my work. This was the first time I have ever heard of a person being tortured in front of a senior police officer. They also beat me. The next day I was taken into interrogation in one of the rooms by a junior police officer. He pointed his revolver at my temple and threatened to kill me. He asked me about my links to the militants: "Give me the weapons! Give me the wireless set!" I was beaten with lathis and kicked and punched. Then they hung me from the ceiling. They tied my hands behind my back with a rope, they put the rope through a pulley in the ceiling, then they pulled the table on which I was standing out from underneath me. Then they used electricity as I was hanging. They did this four times; the fourth time I lost consciousness. When I came to, I was on the floor. I couldn't move my arms, which were behind my back, so two policemen kicked my back to get me to move my arms. Then they returned me to my cell. The next day the torture was lighter. They used the roller on my thighs, and they punched me and threatened me with a pistol, and they told me: "Unless you tell us something about your involvement, you will not get out of here." I gave them the names of all the militants I knew, and told them anything else I knew: the connections I had with human rights people, etc. This situation continued for ten days.

After that, R. was held for an additional five days during which he was lectured not to continue his human rights activities. He was then transferred to a police station where an FIR was registered against him charging him with propagation against the state of India because of his human rights work. The next day he was granted bail, but he was not physically released that day. The SOG had recommended that R. be held under the Public Safety Act, a preventive detention law that permits detention without trial for two years, but the senior state police officer cleared the bail order, and R. was released on February 25. Under the bail order, R. was required to remain in Srinagar. R. told Human Rights Watch that after his release, he stopped his human rights work.

Harassment of Ghulam Nabi Shaheen and Ghulam Rasul Dar

On the night of August 11, 1998, Ghulam Nabi Shaheen, secretary general of the Jammu and Kashmir Bar Association, and Ghulam Rasul Dar, another human rights activist, were detained at Indira Gandhi International Airport in New Delhi as they were preparing to travel to Geneva to attend the meeting of the United Nations Sub-Commission on Prevention of Discrimination and Protection of Minorities. Immigration officials at the airport confiscated their travel documents and interrogated them about their human rights work and their political views. They were permitted to leave only after their flight had departed. Shaheen told Human Rights Watch that in response to international pressure, he was ultimately given permission to travel, but by that time the U.N. meetings had ended.

Attacks on the Press

Although the press in Kashmir reports on some incidents of abuse by government security forces, many newspapers practice self-censorship because they fear reprisals by the security forces or countermilitant groups. In1995 and 1996, several journalists were killed and others injured in violent attacks by countermilitants. The press in Kashmir has also been a frequent target of threats by militant groups.

An incident on June 27, 1997, journalists covering a the arrest of several demonstrators in front of the UNMOGIP building in Srinagar were beaten by police.

Surinder Singh Oberoi of Agence France Press told Human Rights Watch that Superintendent of Police Mubariq Ganai questioned him, "What are you doing here?" Oberoi stated:

When I told him I was performing my professional duty, he put his stick on my shoulder against my neck and said: "Get lost!" I said to him, "Don't use force. If you want me to go, just tell me to go, and I'll go." And I pushed his stick away. Then he started beating me, as did all of his security people with their rifle butts. It's like they had been waiting to pound on all the photographers and were now taking out their wrath on me.

A number of other journalists were also beaten, including Zafar Mehraj of the daily *Kashmir Monitor,* who was later treated at the hospital for his injuries.

After the incident, a large number of local journalists decided to ask for a meeting with Chief Minister Farooq Abdullah to protest. Although any accredited journalist with a press card is permitted to visit any government building, the guards outside the secretariat building refused to allow them to enter and opened fire into the air. The journalists waited outside the gate for two hours before the chief minister came out. He criticized the security forces and apologized to the journalists. He invited them into the conference room and listened as they described what had happened. Oberoi stated:

I told my story, and he apologized to me and said he would order an inquiry. Then Chief Secretary Ashok Jaitley came in a bit later and said: "Why are you making a scene? We said there would be an inquiry, and so there will be." We told him that we wanted an impartial inquiry, and we asked that the three officers concerned be "attached" [i.e., transferred to elsewhere in the city], as they might otherwise try to influence the inquiry. R. Singh, the secretary to Farooq Abdullah, agreed that the three would be attached. And in fact they were transferred, but no inquiry ever took place. I am still waiting. About six months ago, when I raised the matter at another press conference, Farooq Abdullah said that an inquiry was in progress. But until now, nobody has come to me.

When questioned about the incident, Chief Secretary Jaitley stated, "As far as I know, the officer involved was punished, and there was a departmental inquiry." If that were the case, then the inquiry proceeded without the involvement of the key witness and can hardly be considered either impartial or thorough; the case illustrates the government's failure to take appropriate action even in regard to less serious abuse.

In another incident, on July 26, 1997, Habibullah Nakash, a photographer, was beaten by a STF officer during a visit by Indian Prime Minister Inder K. Gujral. He suffered a swollen eye and facial bruises. Oberoi stated:

We all decided to complain, but Jaitley and others begged us not to raise the issue. That evening we went to the press conference for the prime minister and I stood up and said that I wanted to make an appeal concerning a colleague who had been beaten, and could he please intervene. Before I could even finish my short speech, Farooq Abdullah stood up and said: "Who beat the photographer?" I said that it was STF officers. Farooq Abdullah said: "I will suspend them now. If found guilty, I'll dismiss them from the service." He said this in front of everyone, including the prime minister of India. The STF officers were neither suspended nor dismissed, and there was no inquiry.

The Ongoing Problem of Impunity

Government officials have long claimed that security personnel in Kashmir have been disciplined for abuses. When Human Rights Watch met with Chief Secretary Ashok Jaitley on October 20, 1998, he expressed concern about reports of human rights violations, particularly custodial killings. He acknowledged, however, that while disciplinary action was taken against security personnel involved in large massacres in the mid-1990s, no prosecutions take place. He stated:

We ask the army and BSF for reports about incidents and allegations of violations, and people are punished. But it is disciplinary action only; it's impossible to prosecute in a court of law, as no witness will step forward.

What action is taken is not made public.

Major P. Purushottam, public relations officer for the Indian army, described the army's internal monitoring procedures:

We have institutionalized the monitoring of human rights violations by establishing human rights cells at core headquarters and divisional headquarters. These cells carry out their own investigations even if no complaint is lodged. Moreover, new units coming to the valley now receive a three-week pre-induction training course in human rights. The people here are our own people. They must be treated with respect.

We use the Delhi-based newspapers as a basis for starting an investigation of reported human rights violations. At a grassroots level, a certain amount of perceived violations happen. People say they have been roughed up...The delivery of the military system of justice in human rights violations is very fast and very harsh. We use it as a deterrent.

He provided the following examples:

In 1996 in Anantnag, four *jawans* [soldiers] were convicted of gangraping a woman. The jawans were tried in a military court, court-martialed, and given the maximum sentence of ten years rigorous imprisonment in a civil jail. They were also dismissed from the service. If we had allowed this case to go to a civil court, it could have dragged on for ten-fifteen years. We do it in one year: We are the fastest in the world. The second case occurred in Kargil in mid-1997:

A jawan was caught andwithin six months convicted of rape. He was given a sentence of seven years rigorous imprisonment and dismissed from the service. These are criminal acts.

In the past, the Indian government has made public a number of prosecutions of members of security forces for rape. However, even these amount to no more than a handful; many other incidents of rape have never been prosecuted, and reports of rape and other sexual assaults in Kashmir persist. In many cases, these incidents are seldom investigated by judicial and medical authorities competent to determine culpability. In addition, other abuses, particularly torture and extrajudicial execution are rarely investigated. Human Rights Watch is not aware of a single prosecution in a case of the torture or summary execution of a detainee in the ten years since the conflict began.

Human Rights Watch interviewed members of the State Human Rights Commission (SHRC), including Justice Ghulam Ahmad Kuchhay, chairman of the commission. The commission began its work in January 1998 and by November 1998 had undertaken investigations in some 200 cases. Many of these involved complaints unrelated to human rights violations, including salary disputes and environmental concerns.

As is the case with India's National Human Rights Commission, the SHRC has limited powers: its recommendations are not binding, and it does not take up cases pending before the High Court. Although it can undertake an investigation on its own, it cannot directly investigate abuses carried out by the army or other federal forces. However, the commission can summon a representative from these agencies to report about the incident in question. At the time of the Human Rights Watch interview in October 1998, the commission had yet to make public its findings on any human rights case and it was too soon to say whether the commission would provide a significant check on abuses by the security forces.

The Andrabi Killing

The murder of Jalil Andrabi, a human rights lawyer and a leading member of the JKLF, illustrates the impotence of Kashmir's judicial institutions and the fraudulence of the government's claim that it has ensured greater accountability from its forces in Kashmir. The killing attracted international scrutiny and criticism largely because Andrabi was well known, a frequent caller at diplomatic missions in New Delhi, the U.N. Human Rights Commission, and the U.S. State Department. Outside pressure succeeded in forcing the government to conduct an investigation that ultimately indicted the army officer who detained Andrabi and apparently handed him over to be killed. But the officer has not been arrested. When Human Rights Watch interviewed Chief Secretary Ashok Jaitley about the Andrabi case, he acknowledged that it was "a bad case."

On March 8, 1996, Andrabi was detained in Srinagar by Maj. Avtar Singh, known as "Bulbul" (nightingale), of the 35th Rashtriya Rifles unit of the Indian army. Andrabi's wife was told repeatedly by senior police officials that Andrabi was in custody and would be released. Three weeks later, Andrabi's body was found floating in the Jhelum river; an autopsy showed that he had been killed days after his arrest. According to local sources, after his arrest, he was handed over to a countermilitant group to be killed, and the five men responsible were shot dead by Indian security forces a month later. Widespread international condemnation of Andrabi's killing prompted Indian authorities to initiate an investigation that ultimately indicted Maj. Avtar Singh. The High Court ordered Major Singh to appear before the court, but state counsel claimed in response that Singh was not a member of the armed forces but of the "Territorial Army," an irregular force that is under contract with the army, and that his contract had expired and he was nowhere to be found. The bar association has been unable to obtain further information because the case has been filed with the Register Judicial of the High Court and is open to only the court and the state counsel, not to the counsel for Andrabi's family-a highly unusual procedure. Because the case remained pending before the High Court, as of June 1999 the State Human Rights Commission had not conducted any investigation of its own.

Militant Abuses in the Valley

Throughout the conflict, militant organizations in Kashmir have committed grave abuses. The most serious of these have been the murders of hundreds of civilians, both Muslim and Hindu, who have been targeted because of their suspected support for the Indian government, or because they otherwise opposed the policies or practices of one or another of the militant groups. Many of the attacks were also clearly intended to drive Hindu Kashmiris out of the state. Beginning in 1988, Hindus were made the targets of threats and acts of violence by militant organizations, and this wave of killing and harassment motivated many to leave the valley. There are no accurate statistics on the numbers of these killings and other abuses, but anecdotal evidence from Kashmir indicates that they number in the thousands. As of June 1999, thousands of Hindus who fled Kashmir remained in camps in Jammu and Delhi where they have faced serious hardship in finding employment and educational opportunities.

Militants have also abducted and threatened civilians for the purposes of extortion. Members of some of the groups have committed rape, have threatened and attacked journalists, and have kidnapped tourists and others as political hostages. Although political leaders aligned with militant groups have acknowledged that the abuses take place, they have done little, if anything, to curb the abuses.

The militants procure most of their weapons from Pakistan. Although many long-time observers of the region believe that Pakistan has directly provided weapons to militants in Kashmir, there are many complexities about the arms supply relationship. Most of these weapons have come from the arms bazaar in Pakistan's Northwest Frontier Province (nwfp)-a vast black market for weapons-and members of Pakistan's Inter-Services Intelligence (isi), operating either on their own or with the tacit or explicit complicity of the central Pakistani government. The ISI has also operated training camps for Kashmiri militants, some of which have been situated in Afghanistan.

Attacks on civilians have continued. The following examples are illustrative; there have been many more such killings than we describe below. In one of the worst incidents of this kind, on January 26, 1998, militants massacred twenty-three Hindu villagers, including a number of women and children, in the village of Wandhama, seventeen miles north of Srinagar. The village is within the home district of the state chief minister, Farooq Abdullah, and the killings occurred on the Indian national holiday of Republic Day. The militants also set fire to a Hindu temple and a house. On March 21, 1997, seven Hindus were killed in the village of Sangrampora in Badgam district. On August 2, 1998, militants shot dead thirty-four Hindu laborers in a village in the state of Himachal Pradesh near the border with Jammu and Kashmir.

The Applicable International Law

Human Rights Law

International human rights law prohibits the arbitrary deprivation of life under any circumstances. The government of India is a party to the International Covenant on Civil and Political Rights (ICCPR). Article 6 of the ICCPR expressly prohibits derogation from the right to life. Thus, even during time of emergency, "[n]o one shall be arbitrarily deprived of his life."

The ICCPR also prohibits torture and other forms of cruel, inhuman and degrading treatment. Articles 4 and

7 of the ICCPR explicitly ban torture, even in times of national emergency or when the security of the state is threatened.

The Indian army, Special Task Force, Border Security Force, and state-sponsored paramilitary groups and village defence committees-the principal government forces operating in Jammu and Kashmir have systematically violated these fundamental norms of international human rights law. Under international law, India's state-sponsored militias are state agents and therefore must abide by international human rights and humanitarian law. The government of India is ultimately responsible for their actions.

International Humanitarian Law

International humanitarian law, also known as the laws of war, apply when there is a situation of international and internal "armed conflict." Although Human Rights

Watch has maintained that the struggle in Kashmir in the early 1990s did meet this threshhold, it is less clear that international humanitarian law applies to the conflict given the dimunition of fighting throughout much of Kashmir apart from the Kargil region, and the decreased capacity of the militant groups to conduct effective military operations. However, the fact that in Doda and in other border regions militant forces regularly engage Indian army troops, and the size of the armed forces deployed on both sides, suggests that international humanitarian law may still apply.

The international humanitarian law applicable to the conflict in Kashmir is found in Article 3 common to the four Geneva Conventions of August 12, 1949-known as "Common Article 3." Common Article 3 provides international law and standards governing the conduct of parties in an internal armed conflict, including government forces and insurgents. Common Article 3 provides that:

(1) Persons taking no active part in the hostilities, including members of armed forces who have laid down their arms and those placed hors de combat by sickness, wounds, detention, or any other cause, shall in all circumstances be treated humanely, without any adverse distinction founded on race, color, religion or faith, sex, birth or wealth, or any other similar criteria.

To this end, the following acts are and shall remain prohibited at any time and in any place whatsoever with respect to the above-mentioned persons:

(a) violence to life and person, in particular murder of all kinds, mutilation, cruel treatment and torture; (b) taking of hostages; (c) outrages upon personal dignity, in particular humiliating and degrading treatment; (d) the passing of sentences and the carrying out of executions without previous judgment pronounced by a regularly constituted court, affording all the judicial guarantees which are recognized as indispensable by civilized peoples.

(2) The wounded and sick shall be collected and cared for.

However, Common Article 3 in no way precludes the government of India from punishing persons for crimes under its domestic laws. Indeed, Human Rights Watch believes that it is the Indian government's duty to do so. Thus, Kashmiri militants may be tried for murder, kidnapping or other crimes, so long as they are afforded the rights of due process.

Persons protected by Common Article 3 of the Geneva Conventions include all noncombatants, even if they have provided food, shelter or other partisan support to one side or the other, and members of the armed forces of either side who are in custody, are wounded or are otherwise hors de combat. If under these circumstances, such persons are summarily executed or die as a result of torture, their deaths are tantamount to murder.

Torture, hostage-taking, and rape have all been prominent abuses in the Kashmir conflict, and it is evident that Common Article 3 forbids each of them. Rape also violates the ICCPR and Common Article 3 prohibitions on torture.

www.ingramcontent.com/pod-product-compliance
Lightning Source LLC
Chambersburg PA
CBHW021104080526
44587CB00010B/380